MORE
POWER
TEACHING

More Practical Tips for
Surviving and Enjoying
Your Job

Even Though You Teach Adolescents

By Benjamin Mahle

Good Apple
A Division of Frank Schaffer Publications, Inc.

Editors: Janet Barker, Kristin Eclov, Michael Batty, Christine Hood
Cover and Inside Design: Stephanie Villet Berman

Good Apple
A Division of Frank Schaffer Publications, Inc.
23740 Hawthorne Boulevard
Torrance, CA 90505-5927

Contents

Author's Note

At Promontory Point, Utah, a drama about the historic union of two railroads is re-enacted several times a day. Replicas of two great locomotives used during the "golden spike" era are stoked into action. Each locomotive blows its great whistle while chugging along a half-mile track. The ground shudders as the two great engines rumble toward each other before hissing to a stop.

The scene I have just described has everything that I love—great, powerful engines, bells and whistles, grinding passion, and the huge western sky. Utah is a spectacular and diverse amalgam of sky, mountains, canyons, arches, and fleeing landscapes. I could see myself living there and driving one of those trains. That would be my dream job. Next to teaching.

Given the choice between conducting a train or conducting a classroom full of adolescents, I'd choose the latter. Because teaching, you see, is a different adventure every day. It is the best job in the world!

BENJAMIN MAHLE

Day One: First Things First

To illustrate my belief in the power of teaching, I offer the following essay, written in 1992 by one of my ninth-grade students. The essay, penned on the first day of school, appears exactly as it was presented to me. I've purposely made no grammatical or spelling changes. Read past the errors, however, and you'll discover why I'm passionate about teaching adolescents.

"The Incredable good Time"

by Rob

It all happened today. It was time for study hall and we had to go over the rules and regulations of the school and of Miss Vanguard's clas, so she gave us the rule' sheet and commenced talking about the school rules. WEll, I had heard this rap two times already and she was going on and on and I was getting bored so I took the class rules sheet and started playing with it by changeing rules from DO NOT TALK OUT OF TURN to TALK OUT OF TURN and DO NOT THROW ANY OBJECTS to THROW ANY OBJECTS. I could hardly keep from cracking up, especially with my favorite which I changed from: CONSIDER THE WINDOW LEDGE OUT OF BOUNDS. THE WINDOWS ARE THE TEACHER'S RESPONSIBILITY; YOU MAY NOT OPEN OR CLOSE THEM WITHOUT THE TEACHER'S PERMISSION. I changed that to CONSIDER THE WINDOW LEDGE. WINDOWS ARE RESPONSABLE AND YOU MAY OPEN OR CLOSE THEM WITHOUT THE TEACHER'S PERMISSION. And then under REQUIRED MATERIALS I changed LIBRARY BOOKS to MAD LIB books. I had the time of my life.

Rigid teachers may not agree with my, or Rob's, sense of humor, but I thought his essay was funny. Who would have thought that a First Day of School Rules sheet could elicit such comedy? Certainly, I didn't.

Think about it:—After three months away from students, we greet them with a slate of *Dos* and *Don'ts* that would humble or anger anyone. Our well-intended rules strip them of their eager studenthood and make them feel like prison inmates. But that's what most of us have been trained to do—give students rules so we can assert our authority. Rules let students know that we, the teachers, are in control.

My philosophy about teaching is a little different than what you may have learned in graduate school or picked up while student teaching.

I have one rule: "Be appropriate." But I don't tell them that on the first day of school.

Instead, I say:

Hi, I'm Mr. Mahle. That's what I like to be called. When I go through this class list and assign your seats, please correct me if I mispronounce your name. Names are important. I want to call you what you like to be called, unless it's "Meathead" or "Dork," or something you might have used a few years ago to get a laugh out of the class. Oh yes. I have one rule. I'll tell you tomorrow.

And I do.

When I send my Classroom Rules Sheet home with my students, I make it a required assignment. I give it a healthy point value and ask students and parents to acknowledge my expectations by signing the paper at the bottom and returning that portion to me. Doing this within a day or two earns bonus points for the student, and return of the

signed slip proves that a student's parents are also my allies. Don't underestimate the leverage this kind of mini-contract can have, and don't be afraid to follow-up with a phone call if the slip is not returned with a parent's signature.

Mr. Sullivan? This is Wally's English teacher.

No, I haven't had any problems with Wally.

I'm calling to ask if he brought home the sheet that covers my expectations for him in English 9. It's important that you and Wally get a chance to discuss these and let me know if you think any are unreasonable.

Yes. Wally was supposed to have you sign the bottom section after you'd discussed the expectations.

Sure, I have extras; I'll send another with him tomorrow.

Thanks for your time.

On the second day, I ask students to write a definition of *appropriate*. Almost without exception, each person has an idea of *appropriate* that you can live with quite comfortably, for example:

Doin' the right thing at the right time.

Being good when the teacher is talking.

Not distracting others or goofing off.

Knowing right from wrong, and behaving like you know.

And my favorite from the beginning of this last school year:

My deffinision of Appropriate is an act not destructive. Something you can do or say in public without getting a dirty look from someone.

I keep each student's definition on file. If there is ever a question about the child's ability to understand *appropriate*, I can refer back to his or her own thoughtful and accurate definition. I contend that students make choices while fully aware of the appropriateness of their behavior. Having proof of a student's understanding eliminates, in most cases, the "I didn't know it was wrong" response.

Since most students are curious about grading, I explain my grading method on the first day. I show them how they are being credited for cooperating and paying attention. Some years I've also used a Personal Profile Survey (pages 12 and 13), which helps me see the individuality of each student.

This year, on day one, I gave each student a blank seating chart and asked him or her to find his or her assigned seat. Next, they were asked to locate and speak with every other student and to learn his or her name. Then, they had to write their classmates' names in the spaces representing each person's desk.

They then had to find out something that each student liked, which isn't in everyone else's Top Ten, you know, like pizza. I wanted them to find out unique likes such as squid, banjo music, the smell of paint, or mud squishing between toes.

After they were done exchanging names and information, they were asked to add their own names to their seating charts.

This activity, done on a horribly sticky September day, was great for moving kids around,

but more importantly, it encouraged respect for diverse tastes. Our classroom became acquainted in a way that urged cooperation. It was a good beginning, if not a totally "incredible good time."

Day Two: The Rule

On the second day, I explain my one rule and a few expectations. Perhaps you are thinking that my "expectations" are actually rules stripped of *Dos* and *Don'ts*. If so, you've got me. Kids catch on too, but they don't see the difference between rules and expectations so much as *feel* it. Saying "expectations" suggests that students have the intelligence and endurance to live up to what is required for them to succeed. Youngsters aren't compelled then—as Rob was—to rewrite rules as a way to protest being told things that anyone with the intellect of a cabbage already understands.

I think most of us use rules to remind ourselves, not the students, that we are in charge. This often marks us as opponents. However, when we write our "rules" as "expectations," we impress students with just how much we feel they are capable of doing. We become their *allies*, and our jobs become about *surveying* and *nurturing* progress while encouraging *self-control*.

After students have had a chance to review the rules sheet, I ask: "OK, who has a question?"

A flurry of hands go up.

Why can't we sit where we want?

Well, what if you all wanted the same seat? Can't you imagine what a riot it would be with everybody wanting this seat here, closest to my desk? And what about learning your names? It would take me weeks. And if we had a sub—heaven forbid you should ever be without me—well, that person would need a seating chart. And what if you thought you wanted to sit next to someone and it turned out they didn't really want you next to them, think how embarrassing THAT could be, and then what if you really wanted to sit next to someone but were too shy to arrange that; well, maybe you'd actually be assigned to sit next to them. Talk about a dream come true. And . . .

OK, OK, OK, already.

Other questions?

What's the deal about having to sit in our seats when you dismiss us, and then we have to follow you out of the room?

I know, I know—it sounds like some kind of big power thing, some authority deal, doesn't it?

Sounds like we're in second grade.

Right. Let me explain. You see, the school I was at before this one had carpeted halls, and our custodian, Tiny, who was about seven feet and 300 pounds—well, he used to run this zamboni-type sweeper down the hall, and one day he was coming past with his machine and one of my kids scampered out ahead of me—I didn't have this "me first" policy then—and danged if he didn't get sucked right into that machine.

Yeah, right.

What's more, I've learned that when a person first enters the hall there is a slight stirring of air. Sometimes that turbulence will send a stray virus heading his or her way. I am there to intercept that virus before it can infect any of you. I'll do that for you, because I care. It's my job to keep you safe. And I take my job seriously.

Heads shake side to side, small grins play over some faces.

If you don't believe me, ask Rachel Horn.

Who's she?

A student I had last year. She snuck past me one time, and the next day she came down with a cold, followed by a cold sore under her nose the size of a straberry, just before the winter dance. You can ask her. So I have to be the first one out the door. I owe it to you.

You don't owe students explanations for everything. But I've found that if I blend truth with my corny, personal fiction, it takes the edge off things I ask kids to do. There's power in being a lunatic—It commands attention and enables me to be heard.

THE RULE AND EXPECTATIONS

THE RULE:

BE APPROPRIATE

EXPECTATIONS:

● Be in the room and either seated or near your desk when the period is to begin.

● Please bring all necessary materials to class. These include the following:
  — Three-ring binder for English handouts
  — College-rule spiral notebook
  — 40 to 70 pieces of lined paper—to be used only for English
  — Pencil with an eraser
  — Pen
  — Appropriate reading material as assigned

● You are expected to attempt all assignments; expect some homework too.

● Plan to spend the full period on English (reading, writing, vocabulary, and so on).

● Please ask for help when you need more information and when you have not been able to figure things out.

● Make your work area clean and help put your row in order before leaving.

● Please remove hats when entering the room.

● We will dismiss from assigned seats. Expect me to be the first to leave the room each day.

● Expect to be successful: Regular attendance, finishing homework, and staying on task will earn you a passing grade in my class.

● Do not expect re-takes on tests.

● If you want more help, I will be glad to work with you.

● Expect to be asked frequently to read, to write, and to think. You will become happier as your skill with language increases. Thinking is hard work, but doing hard work shows you are growing and maturing as a person.

REMEMBER THE RULE.

Detach here. Sign and return the lower portion. Retain the top portion.

- -

We have read and discussed the rule and expectations and believe they are reasonable.

Student's signature _____ Parent's signature _____

Phone No.(s) _____ Date _____

Personal Profile

Caring about kids is the easiest way to care about your job. For most of us, caring about each student as a person is easier when we are able to distinguish one student from another. This means we must learn their names.

I use a Personal Profile Sheet (pages 12 and 13) to help me attach a name to some detail of a student's life. I can better remember "Bobby Simonson, whose home smells like bleach," than I can remember "Bobby Simonson, ninth grader."

Most students willingly complete the Personal Profile Sheet. It gives each of them a chance to share something that makes him or her different from the child in the seat ahead.

Information from this tool also helps me recognize opportunities. When Ginny writes that her least favorite class is English, I will be certain to greet her the next morning with a compliment and use her name: "Cool shirt, Ginny."

Sometimes I am able to anticipate problems: Fred writes, *Three people from the past I'd like to meet are Dracula, Jeffrey Dahmer, and Jack the Ripper* and *My favorite hobby is irritating teachers.* Fred probably enjoys getting a rise out of teachers, or adults generally. But he may have a fascination with the macabre that bears watching. He may need to see that I will listen to his non-conformist views and reserve comment on his outlandish tastes. He may simply want my attention or may be testing to see if I'll shrug him off. The profile raises interesting questions that I enjoy looking into.

The Profile may also give me a baseline of where each student is beginning the year in terms of his or her attitude toward school, toward my particular class, and toward life in general.

Grade Level _____   Date _____

PERSONAL PROFILE SHEET

(3 possible points)
Dream up some cool answers to the following questions.
Remember, neatness counts too!

1. My full name is _____

and I like to be called _____.

My birth date was _____.

2. My parent's names are _____.

3. Something about me that is interesting which my teachers will probably remember is

_____

_____.

4. My address is _____
(Street)

_____
(City, State, Zip)

Phone: _____   E-Mail: _____

5. I have _____ brothers and _____ sisters (include half- and step-).

6. My pets are _____.

7. My hobbies or interests outside of school are _____

_____

_____.

8. My favorite subject is _____ because _____

_____.

9. My least favorite subject is _____ because _____

_____.

10. In this class I expect _____

_____.

11. My best skills are _____

_____.

12. If my family were a noise it would sound like _____ .

13. Three people from history that I'd like to meet are _____ ,
_____ , and _____ .

14. Three people who are still alive that I'd like to meet are _____ ,
_____ , and _____ .

15. The smell that best describes my home is _____ .

16. The animal I most resemble right now is a (an) _____

because _____

_____ .

17. The color that best shows how I usually feel is _____ .

I chose this because _____ .

18. If I could have anything I wanted, it would be _____

because _____ .

19. The thing I would most like to change in this world is _____

because _____

_____ .

20. If I could live anywhere I liked, I would choose to live in _____

because _____ .

21. At this point, I would give my life the following grade: (circle one)

A+   A   B+   B   C+   C   D   F

22. Write anything here that might help me understand you and work with you better. (This part is optional.)

_____

_____

_____

_____

_____

_____

Seven Attributes of True Attitude and Power

Last night, I watched a great high school talent: an all-state point guard from a Minneapolis school. I watched him single-handedly break down the opposing team's defenses with his quickness and deft shooting touch. He scored 35 points on slashing drives to the hoop, fall-away jump shots, looping three-pointers, layups off steals he'd made, and foul shots. He exasperated his opponents time and again, dribbling through two or three defenders or dishing passes to wide-open teammates on the few occasions his path to the basket was stalled. Everyone in the arena marveled at his physical skills, but only his mother could have liked him much.

The first time he handled the ball, he stopped play and complained to the official that the ball was underinflated. He slumped his shoulders, grimaced, and made quite an effort at sustaining a pained look. The confounded official checked the lad's complaint, but the ball seemed to bounce fine. The game proceeded but was marked by brief delays, including a particularly flashy move by the star who raised his hand, signed a "V," then twirled his fingers as though fluffing an imaginary hairdo. Several times he drifted to the sideline for congratulations from the team mascot or to gesture to acquaintances in the stands. The topper came after he made a remarkable shot while falling down. Instead of appearing at the free throw line, he sprinted to his benched teammates and gave them all high fives. The perplexed referee waited for his return, as did the entire crowd.

Upon exiting the arena, my 85-year-old father offered the understatement of the night: "I found him kinda hard to take." What we found disgusting was not the athlete's confidence or his domination of the opponent. What we found distasteful was how his self-adulation had corrupted his persona and soiled his remarkable talents. Someone had spoiled him rotten. For lack of a better term, what stunk most about him was his attitude. Still, major colleges are courting this player despite his having failed the same college entrance proficiency test six times.

Don't get me wrong—I like "attitude"—the attitude that doesn't just shout, "Look at me!" I like the attitude that *demands* because it wants to know more, is *impatient* because it wants to do more, and *pushy* because it wants others to be more than they are currently satisfied with being. True attitude is spirit and optimism and creativity and love. At times it may touch a bit roughly on the borders of another person's sanctuary, but it does not demand to be let in. This attitude may startle you, even annoy you a bit; but "true" attitude always goes beyond self-aggrandizement and nudges others to do better. And, a part of true attitude is listening and being willing to respond, "Okay. I'll change a little if you will."

ONE A "Common" Sense Approach

Eight years ago, while on sabbatical leave from teaching junior high school, I wrote *Power Teaching* (originally published by Fearon Teacher Aids and now published in a revised edition by Good Apple, 1999). This book was predicated on the notions of "right" and "reasonable" as applied to all aspects of teaching, but especially with regard to managing student behavior. Though I didn't think of it as such at the time, this book attempted to deal with attitudes, including some of my own.

Today, managing student behavior—and tolerating it at times—is still our single greatest challenge and concern. It requires, above all, common sense. I worry that my attitude may sometimes blur my vision of "common" sense, especially when administrative educational philosophies suddenly seem like "non"-sense, or when teachers fall under criticism for failing to teach Johnny to read, write, and compute, especially when Johnny has spent most of his time shooting baskets and being adored for the high percentage of them that drop through the net. The media, too, seems delighted to present examples of students who *can't* and schools that *don't*. These become the subject of "Special Reports," which often highlight statistics that show that teachers come from the lowest-achieving 20 percent of all college graduates. (Maybe there's something to that—If we were really smart, we'd be making big money as computer engineers or corporate lawyers instead of helping kids develop the knowledge to assume those roles.) There is always plenty of blame to go around—parents are being targeted more heavily now—but little seems to fall to the students themselves. In some ways this is good. I'd prefer that we don't blame students. But each of us should challenge student attitudes that say, "Accept me just like I am, and give me what I want regardless. Adapt to me. I can't learn or change, and moreover, I don't need to."

In the late 1980s, administrators scrambled to find new systems of educational delivery. School boards enacted policies of teacher accountability that they hoped would insulate them against lawsuits from disgruntled parents whose children had graduated but couldn't read *TV Guide*. The popular notion was that teachers needed to be better trained—Each of us needed more classroom hours outside of our work day in order to (first) *recognize dysfunctional students* and (second) *learn how to "fix" them.* None of this hubbub suggested that having more teachers, more parental involvement, or better student preparation might improve student performance. Rather, the fault was with teachers for not recognizing and adapting to kids' different learning styles. If teachers knew what to do—and would bother doing it—each shy, budding genius would ultimately burst into glorious, iridescent bloom.

It was simple—Each of us merely needed to build individual plans of strategy for each child's needs.

Indeed. I'd want an analysis of individual needs and learning style for my own child. However, I wouldn't expect any teacher to factor in my child's attitude. Attitude is largely choice, born of the urge for immediate gratification, which, if satisfied often enough—usually at the expense of others—tends to take on the hue of entitlement. We disarm our kids of empathy, compassion, tolerance, and grace when we allow self-gratification to overwhelm all of an individual's other responsibilities to him- or herself. Self-improvement, self-discipline, self help, and self-discovery are but a few of the "selfs" that suffer when we excuse bad manners, rationalize poor choices, and dispense unearned praise and rewards.

TWO Teaching and Learning

A teacher ought to be learning as much each day as he thinks he is teaching to us; if he is not, he is a fool.

An eighth grader named Kitty wrote that to me on the last day of my first teaching year 27 years ago. She had attitude, but one for which I'm grateful.

Attitude can improve teaching as well as learning. Teachers are given learning opportunities every minute, and I pity colleagues who refuse to invest in change. Much research has been done on learning styles and how to accommodate individual differences. We can always do better, and should welcome new strategies that work for kids—more so if we're given time to learn them. Still, most of what we need to learn about managing kids takes place in the classroom. Learning from students is the fastest way to become more effective.

Like it or not, students often teach us through naughty and mischievous behavior. Most of these lessons are rooted not in psychological angst or improper nutrition, but in our weak expectations for kids. We should make it clear to each of them early on what we expect. Our expectations are the clearest signal to others of our attitudes, and these must support our right to teach and the right of kids to be taught. Otherwise we are destined to

fail, regardless of all we know about learning styles and building self-esteem, or about which colors in a room pacify and which provoke.

Little disruptive behavior emanates from kids who aren't sure of how civilized human beings are supposed to act; this behavior usually comes from kids who don't understand the premium we put on civility.

THREE Hats and Language

The expectation of *civility* is still being debated. For instance:

Is it civil to expect kids not to wear hats in school?
Is it civil to expect kids to use language that is free of profanity and does not demean the personalities of others?
Are we too austere if youngsters can't wear what they want and say what they feel when they feel like saying it?

Some people will argue that our expectations are too stern, that we blunt the creative spirit and the spontaneity of kids if we insist that they think before speaking or remove a hat before entering school. I feel strongly that language and dress have huge practical and symbolic applications in defining the climate—the attitude, if you will—of the school.

A young colleague said to me, "Hats? Don't we have bigger issues than hats to worry about?" Yes. But hats are one thing we can do something about. I allowed hats to be worn one year in my classroom. By the end of the first semester I still couldn't identify some of the boys who wore hats or who didn't on a rare day. The hats gave them a kind of undifferentiated birdlike look with shadows for eyes. And hats were a favorite thing for other students to nab or steal. It was difficult, at times, to take seriously students wearing gaudy or sweat-stained hats that hid their eyes. What next, sunglasses?

Worst of all, allowing hats in school let the wearer believe that hats could be worn anywhere, under any circumstances. My final decision against hats came when several ninth-grade students, who had been treated to front-row seats at Minneapolis' State Theater Production of *Joseph and the Amazing Technicolor Dreamcoat*, argued with me and another school sponsor about removing their hats in the theater. A few days later I even saw a young man wearing a hat at his father's memorial service. The following school year, I decided not to allow hats in my room. Hats in school may or not be a major issue, but when a student must remove a hat when entering a school building, it reinforces the idea that school is somehow different from the street— *that school has its own attitude.*

My young friend John also argued against the importance of profanity-free language. "If a student swears at me, that's one thing," he said, "but if he simply swears. . . . "

I agree that cursing at a teacher is different from merely cursing in his or her presence. You should never again suffer a student who swears at you. Swearing after you hit your thumb with a hammer is probably to be expected and can be treated as a one-time-only event. Similarly, I treat those outbreaks that happen in the heat of passion in a different category:

Ah, Janet. I'm sorry that the strap broke on your book bag, but do you think you could talk to it in some other way?

Accidents happen. Irritations, minor and major, elicit swearing. Gentle corrections work best, and most kids expect some form of intervention or response. Even students who are angry with each other can be brought back with a quiet approach, and the damage can be easily repaired as long as no one has been physically attacked or had his or her dignity bruised.

However, to allow casual cursing—to ignore sexually charged language and innuendo, racial or ethnic slurs, or threats—is to invite the worst part of the street into your school. Why do that?

Verbal restraint and inoffensive language are in every person's repertoire. It's true that avoiding profanity requires some thought for some people, usually by those who most need to think. Are we opposed to having kids think? By the age of two, most of us know enough language to ask for what we need. If we are to continue pushing language upon our young, is it not so we can expand their capacity to communicate ideas and feelings in ways that others are most likely to receive them? Offensive speech is not freedom of expression. Rather, it labels and catalogues the speaker. We do a disservice to students when we tolerate "bad" language. Firm guidelines about appropriate language exert a kind of gravity which yanks back the spittle of viciousness and anger and insists that we behave better than hissing cats or snarling dogs. Guidelines remind the habitual or casual swearer that coarse language is a poor substitute for real thought. And really, is it too much to ask that we require our students to employ the entire alphabet here in school?

I think these expectations are a trifling price to pay for the privilege of an education.

FOUR Democracy and Power

I'd guess that if you visited the homes of people opposed to my "austerity," you'd find that in many cases the kids are in charge.

I don't believe in letting kids be in charge. My classroom is not a democracy; it is a benevolent dictatorship. I believe schools should be similarly undemocratic.

This is not to say that we shouldn't encourage kids to invest in the running of a classroom or the governing of a school. Kids need to be heard. Empowering them doesn't mean simply giving them voices; it means listening to them. Young people don't want freedom or equality—they want justice. They want a return on their investment of time and energy. They want to be seen and remembered. They want chances to prove their individual worth. This is an attitude that we need to encourage.

FIVE Miracle Workers If . . .

I believe that we teachers could solve nearly all of the problems in education if only we were given a few things:

School boards who trumpet appropriate behavior for kids and that enthusiastically urge parents to be involved in preparing kids at home.

Colleagues who are willing to learn and change.

Legislators who will make parents and kids more responsible for learning and who appropriate funds to back up the mandates they put on schools.

Administrators with guts—women and men who'll say without apology that "Education is a privilege," and "Our building is not the street," and who believe that with top-down leadership, we can have any kind of school we want!

The attitude needed to challenge requests that undermine our right to teach and the rights of students to learn.

A colleague of mine in another school district was asked to include—in a class of 30 kids—a fifth-grade student who bites, kicks, and sometimes urinates on the floor. Teachers must challenge such requests. Teachers must refuse to participate in such nonsense. Teachers must develop the courage to seek legal recourse if punished for refusing an order that compromises his or her right to teach and the rights of students to learn. Each of us is obliged to do this on our own behalf and that of our students.

Another colleague was criticized for failing too many students. He taught math and graded tests based on the number of correct answers. He told his principal:

Simon is failing because he is only averaging 4 out of 10 on his quizzes.
What is passing?
Six.
Why not lower your curve to four?

By suggesting that the curve be lowered by 20 percent, the principal implied that, somehow, Simon would benefit. I don't see how. If Simon is really trying, there are other creative ways to help him pass, such as assigning other tasks related to the subject areas that don't require computations, memory work, or physical dexterity. Pass Simon when he completes an alternative measurement of knowledge. But please—Let's not teach Simon that 40 percent is 60 percent.

These are not hypothetical examples. Nor are they the rule. I merely mention these things because they have contributed to the development of my attitude.

SIX Whining

Occasionally I whine. For some of us there needs to be a time and a place for whining. Of course, it is never in the teacher's lounge, in your classroom, at a parent conference, or in a public place where we ought to be ambassadors of optimism and enlightenment. But if whining makes you feel better, you may whine once in a while to your spouse, your dachshund, or your colleague over a glass of wine. You may rip and shred the decisions that make your job tough. Vent your disgust with the shortcomings of kids and colleagues and governments and parents and astrological predictions and the weather. Expel those affronts that swell inside you like too much root beer. There is a place for venting: Sometimes it's necessary—Simply refuse to let it be your dominant attitude.

Every now and then I invite my friend Karen for a glass of wine after school, or she invites me. Then we complain. We never fail to enjoy this diversion, which is a rare but necessary component of our mental health. A planned complaint session once every three months or so can prevent the unplanned complaining from becoming commonplace. That is

my view; twist it as you choose. But if you act as I have suggested, don't feel guilty. Take pride in having had the strength and humor not to have acted on these feelings when you might have hurt kids or the staff you meet with every day with the common goal of preparing youngsters for a better life.

SEVEN The Best Job . . .

I know that I have the best job in the world—I'm a teacher. I save lives. I make lives better for kids and their families and the families they will start one day. I do this for so-so pay, a little respect, and at considerable emotional and—at times—physical risk. I am a hero. This is possible partly because I do have an attitude that I walk and talk each day. I choreograph a strut of attitude. I sing, whisper, or shout it to audiences of kids or colleagues or parents—anyone who will watch and listen to my declaration of what is reasonable and right. It is a planned performance that I put on with rehearsed rhetoric and a repertoire of actions that I add to every day as I learn. I sustain my attitude with passion fueled by the respect and affection of kids and by proof of their success.

I hope you don't feel my attitude makes me seem to think I know it all, or never make mistakes, or have this job licked. I am humbled every day by what I don't know—by what I have overlooked—and by even the one person I might fail to help that day. But I don't believe in lingering over what's done; instead, learn, acknowledge your emotions, and move ahead.

One of my ninth-grade students, 15-year-old Tina, illustrates that point in her journal entry, as follows.

It seems like people always find something to complain about. . . . All I ever hear is "I'm too fat, too tall, too ugly —I hate zits, blah, blah, blah." It's all in your mind. You see, if people give you compliments, take them. . . .

I never hear people say how great it is to be alive, to smell cookies baking in the oven, to see spring come and go, to feel your dog slobber you with wet kisses. Why can't people just accept themselves? Everyone has some kind of beauty but if you have inner beauty it kinda grows through you, it shoots out your fingertips and out the edge of your smile; it's the glimmer in your eye. . . .

Students like Tina remind me that I, too, am a student. Education is an ongoing process that both inspires and humbles me. As a teacher, I am constantly learning. It's why I believe . . .

**Teaching
is the best job
in the world!**

Alphabet Kids

Two years ago, I had a student in my class with cerebral palsy. I was very nervous. His case worker said that Greg had limited academic potential (educationalese for being "dumb"), that he occasionally threw tantrums, and that his mother believed he was much smarter than he actually was. He'd been known to plow into people with his power wheelchair. His mother said, "He gets mostly As and Bs, but I think the aide does all his work."

On the first day Greg rolled in early with his aide, smiling.

Hi, I'm Greg.
I'm Mr. Mahle. Nice to meet you.
Me too.

He motored into my room, looked at the back wall, which was mostly covered with multi-colored construction paper, and asked:

What you goin' ta do with that?
We're going to write poems and use that for background to display them.
I like poems.

Greg, it turns out, liked almost everything. He liked video drama, class discussion, and hearing others read aloud. He liked his classmates, the building principal, the CARE van driver, his mom, his little sister and brother, the wide hallways, and writing. At home on his computer, he wrote energetic, comical tales about a frog with super powers. Hour after hour he labored to hunt down letters and poke them out with his gnarled fingers. He produced about one word a minute even while his mind ran miles ahead. When he was done, he printed his tale of Froggman: ten pages in green type.

I know Greg wrote his own stories. His mom worked full-time and was raising two other kids. His dad had left the family. His aide, because of his devotion to Greg, insisted that Greg do everything he could. Greg, by necessity, did his own work. My first lesson from this experience—See things for yourself.

Greg was difficult to understand at first. He spoke loudly in his young man's deepening voice, long liquid vowel sounds pushed by thick consonants. Ten years ago I would have been afraid that Greg would be mocked by his classmates or that I would be helpless in communicating with him. But we underestimate ourselves and our adaptability, and we underestimate the adaptability of kids and especially their good hearts. Greg's presence commanded no more special interest from his classmates than if he'd been left-handed or tall. Until he laughed. Greg applauded things that most kids found amusing, but which they would not feel comfortable laughing about in front of their peers. My stupid clue about spelling *vacuum* is a good example.

How do you remember that vacuum has two us?

No response.

Think about vacuuming, what it sounds like.

To demonstrate, I pushed my loyal Kirby™ vacuum.

Uuuuuuuumh. Uuuuuuuuumh!

Greg loved this corny spelling clue and his great phlemy laugh burst forth. Others laughed too—either at the situation or at Greg's laugh, which he could share without embarrassment. Greg loosened up the entire class with his innocent, unrestrained joy of life. Ten years ago, without knowing the boy, I might have argued against mainstreaming Greg. I would have asked, "Wouldn't he do better one-on-one? Kids will hurt his feelings. What do I do about that?"

What to do? With Greg, as with all students, do what is right—Insist that individuals be respected. I knew that, but didn't want to change anything. A second great lesson is that the mandates we get about mainstreaming often come from people who do know better than we do that change is sometimes for the best.

Among many mainstream teachers, Greg and other kids with special needs are often referred to as *alphabet kids*—youngsters whose behavior is different from most kids', or whose difficulty in learning is the result of a disability that can be proved through testing. We use *alphabet* as an adjective rather than commit to memory the terms behind the acronyms for their disorders: EBD (Emotionally Behaviorally Disordered), EMH (Educable Mentally Handicapped), ADHD (Attention Deficit Hyperactive Disorder), POHI (Physically or Other Handicapped Individual), and so on. We're not insensitive about language and labeling. But *alphabet kids* is the blanket term under which these children are somehow lumped together.

Of course, each special child poses a special problem for the regular classroom teacher. With Greg, the problem was how not to like him too much. Many of us have taught special needs kids, though, who were not as lovable as Greg—kids who gave us nightmares.

It would be nice if each of us viewed problems as opportunities. But it is even better when we can avoid problems and find opportunities in the arena of life provided by good planning and communication, and by weather that will allow us to get our potatoes in early. Greg came at an opportune time in my teaching life. I'd never had a student in a wheelchair. I'd grown too comfortable. His arrival gave me access to a special boy and a special aide. He brightened my room, and I learned that even at age 50, I could expand my range of comfort to include people who can't walk or whose speech requires attentive listening and watching.

But what of those other kids, the EBD and ADHD kids, those whose histories show frequent disruption, who are described informally by their previous teachers as "off the wall"? Do they really come to us so totally wrapped in legalese that we must weigh our every word to them? If they act out, is there anything we can do? Many of us don't seem to think so. And yet, each of these students can potentially enrich a room as much as Greg did. It is fine to include them. We must simply insist that each child *be appropriate*. This can be anticipated by speaking with special education teachers and by our timely attendance at Individual Educational Plan (IEP) meetings.

Every alphabet kid has an IEP. In theory, this plan is written with input from the student, the parents, the special education teacher, the site principal, doctors, counselors, therapists—anyone with a bearing on the child's success—including you, the teacher. If you will have a special needs child in your classroom, you should be advised as to when and where this IEP will be reviewed. Attend those meetings. Raise questions and concerns. Some of the IEPs I have reviewed were written as though the child's teachers were instructional miracle workers. The academic goals, though laudable, would mostly escape the reach of a Rhodes scholar. I believe in optimism. And one can easily trip over the shoelaces of low expectations. But if you have seen this child in action, you should know what is reasonable.

Moreover, IEPs too often fail to address the consequences of misbehavior. This is amazing to me—that the possibility of a student behaving in a way that brought him to have an IEP is mostly ignored. Touchy issues. Better retreat. Don't want to offend anyone. Keep everything upbeat and positive. Well, you can be positive that a student in your class with a history of behavioral problems who is not clear about consequences for his or her behavior will offend someone. These are a few of the reasons you need to be present at an IEP meeting. Realistic academic and behavioral goals need to be reviewed and amended with your input, and consequences for negative behaviors spelled out so the suggestion that "building and district policies will be applied" is at least included.

Throughout this process, you should realize that parents of special needs kids are anxious to hear voices of reason and want to be your allies.

Some may be slow to warm to you—they have often experienced lulls in the system that have seemed unreasonable and standoffish, and they've known teachers to be closed-minded about the "letters" assigned to a child's special needs: "That kid just needs to get more sleep and quit eating so much junk food, and his parents need to unplug the TV and put the kibosh on his computer games."

When given a chance to be heard, these parents will be *advocates* for their child. This, at least, should be your hope. However, they know far better than we the challenges these youngsters present. They often admire the fact that you work with many kinds of students, that you know how to motivate and discipline. They watch you, with hope. Parents are on your side. Attend meetings with them, listen well, and voice your concerns with sound reason, civility, and kindness:

What suggestions can you give me about working with Fred? You know him best.

Well, he's pretty sensitive. He hates the way his handwriting looks, and he can't spell. Try to go easy on him about handwriting.

What kinds of things is he good at doing?

He likes small engines, working with his hands.

Does he have any special interests or activities?

Oh, brother. He has a collection of stuffed animals that would push you out the door. And he loves to paint with watercolors and draw.

We must be sensitive to individual differences and appreciative of them, too. We must recognize that some kids have been dealt a tougher hand. EBD, LD (Learning Disabled), EMH, POHI, ADD (Attention Deficit Disorder), ADHD—these are conditions to reckon with honestly, with compassion, with common sense, and with all available resources.

Lazy

Education has its four-letter words. One of them is *lazy*. There is a fleet of large ears that hover like invisible alien vessels over the parent/teacher conference rooms of every school in this country, just waiting for you to utter the word *lazy*. Educational propriety absolutely forbids the use of this word in describing a student to his parents.

A friend of mine once conferenced with parents despite being in the throes of a terrible head cold. He suddenly sneezed into his hand, then found time moments later to discover a hand-kerchief in his back pocket. Throughout the conference, Tim never once used the word *lazy* to describe these parents' youngster, even though the boy's performance in phys-ed closely resembled that of a garden slug. Tim, in fact, thought he had been kind and subtle, using the term *mysteriously unmotivated* several times, hoping on each occasion that the parents would unlock the "mystery." Still, at the conclusion of the conference, both parents refused to shake Tim's hand.

No matter how he led the conversation away from it, Tim could not hide from the reality of snot on his hand. Even though he'd done his best to remove it, to pretend he hadn't arrested ten billion germs in his palm, the parents knew better. Parents know better.

When you have a student who appears to be lazy, it is unwise to quickly draw this conclusion. But you must describe what you see. Encourage his parents to describe what *they* see. If you have similar views, you might explore with them possible reasons for the child's lack of effort in your class.

So Mr. Abercrombie, Jay hasn't earned a point this quarter. He's been reluctant to bring a pencil to class even on days when I give special "pencil with an eraser" points. And, when asked to write two words to describe the best day of his life he simply shrugged, set aside the pencil I'd lent him, and put his head down on his desk. What would you say about this?

Kid is lazy. Doesn't do a damned thing to help out at home either. I could sprinkle talcum powder under the couch on Saturday morning, and by dinner time, you could see that he hadn't left it even once. His mom and I work our butts off. We don't know what's up with him.

Many people would call this student "lazy." Many educators, playing safe, would call him "unmotivated." I hate that word. A student who thinks he sees the chance to get by with doing nothing has a motive.

A colleague who works with "special education" students prefers the "amotivational" in describing a particular student's lack of involvement in some area of his life. I think the term applies to those persons who are not interested even in finding the path of least resistance.

Concerned parents and educators need to explore a number of possibilities before declaring a youngster "lazy." Depression can cause a child to *appear* to be lazy; many other medical conditions could do the same, and this could be your first suggestion to parents, or a question: "Has Leo had a physical examination?"

It is also okay to ask about his friends, his social life, and his association with chemicals: "You know, the way you've described Ben is the way we sometimes see kids who have become preoccupied with, you know, parties and things? Does he get enough sleep? What is his view on kids who drink or use other drugs?"

Marijuana use is especially insidious in promoting the amotivational malaise.

Teachers must not be shy about suggesting these possibilities to parents. Parents often don't have the information. Some may think their child's "casual" use of potentially addicting chemicals is simple experimentation or "not enough to really hurt." They need to know that the brain of an adolescent is not the brain of an adult. Because of the immaturity of the brain and the endocrine system, an adolescent is likely to develop symptoms of dependency at a rate five times faster than that of an adult. In 18 months or less, an adolescent can go from "social drinker" to alcoholic. Parents need to know that amotivational behavior may be a symptom of serious chemical involvement.

My primary concern in this chapter is not to make excuses for students who appear on any typical day to be lazy. Rather, I am encouraging teacher and parents not to use the word as a "cop out"—as the reason why John or Georgia is not working in class. I especially encourage the teacher who seems to have more than one or two "lazy" students to examine his or her teaching style. Teachers must model the behavior that they want to teach, or they will be teaching something else. A teacher who appears indifferent to, or who detests, teaching grammar will facilitate similar feelings in students if he or she does not find a way to show delight and enthusiasm for this area. Learning to deal good-naturedly with things we dislike is what mature professionals do, and it is exactly what we ask students to do every single day.

Teachers must also consider how their interactions with kids contribute to or detract from a particular student's interest in a subject, and subsequently, his or her effort. The parent who tells you, "He always does well for the teachers that he likes," is really saying, "He really does well for the teachers whom he thinks LIKE HIM!" The old adage "It's better to be respected than liked," is probably wrong. We need to engage kids in ways that help them want to *not* disappoint us.

Many students leave school after years of repeated failure. No doubt some of them were lazy. But others may simply have found that our delivery system is too rarely meshed with the systems they have for receiving information. A visual learner would excel in a class where overheads, films, maps, and graphs were used more than lectures. Certainly a student with auditory deficits could benefit from notes and handouts. The kinesthetic learner would need something to do with his or her hands that applied to learning the subject. Research shows that 80 percent of all high school dropouts have a dominant learning style different from that of most of their teachers. This, then, is a plea for teachers to adopt multi-sensory approaches whenever possible. If a kid has his head down during a lecture, it does not mean he isn't listening, and it's not necessarily proof that he doesn't like your general science class. He very well may have strong auditory skills, and one of those Velcro® minds that catches all those things you are saying and has them stick. Simply ask: "Jim, did you get that explanation of mitosis?"

Personally, I can hear much better with my head down and my eyes closed. Behaviors like this often represent adjustments the child has made in order to connect with information. The proof, of course, will come when you assess the child.

Wonderful progress has been made in recent years in using medications to alleviate the symptoms of ADD and ADHD. The affected student, because of his or her unique brain chemistry, is unable to filter the things you are saying or showing from the hum of the florescent lights, the dumpster truck outside your classroom window, the perfume of the girl behind him or her, or the rustle of papers. The child's apparent indifference to what you want him or her to retain may push the conclusion of "lazy," or even worse, may lead you to believe he or she is selectively lazy by showing interest in so many things you are *not* doing. If such a child has been diagnosed with either of these conditions, you might question if he or she has been prescribed medications, and to ask if those meds are indeed being taken regularly or on schedule. If he or she has not been diagnosed, you need to offer your observations to a counselor or someone who cares. The symptoms of these disorders are not hard to learn, and responsible teachers need to make the effort to recognize them, especially since recent studies show that at least half of all such students benefit from medication.

We are all busy. And students who seem lazy invite our indifference far more easily than students who act out. It is easy to let "lazy" serve as the explanation for a youngster's failure to thrive, especially since parents may fully agree with us.

It is not right to leave the "lazy" student alone. It is reasonable to ask questions and consider the possible impact of chemicals, depres-sion, learning disabilities, the delivery methods we use, our attitude toward the student, and the role modeling of parents, as well as our own.

But what happens when we have explored these other possibilities? What do we do with the youngster who simply *chooses* not to work? I would say our best plan then is simply not to enable them. "Lazy" kids probably became that way because they were clever enough to get others to be in their service. Personally, I will still write a parent about his or her child's under-achievement. I will not harangue, or wring my hands, or take the blame, or dislike the lazy child. What I will do, however, is allow the natural consequences of the child's behavior to fall in the appropriate place.

Perhaps you want to do the same. Make a list of reasonable consequences. Present it to the child in the form of a contract. Review and update the consequence list frequently, and rewrite the contract as the child becomes more or less responsible. I realize this can involve serious amounts of time, but a child's written word carries considerably more weight with him or her and with others who might later become involved in examining his or her behavior and how you have attempted to deal with it. Contracting is a form of documentation, and clarity and brevity are watch words:

James will be on task at least 20 minutes before asking for a lavatory pass.

In exchange for remaining in the class, Fred will report any tardies to his parents and bring a signed note the next day acknowledging this report.

Of course, you only contract for consequences you can apply and for behavior the youngster is capable of performing.

Contracting is a way of positioning a student firmly into the real world. "Yeah, Mr. Mahle, I'll do better" is an oral contract and may very well be genuine. But a brief, written document, signed and dated, is a concrete thing—visible, touchable, and surprisingly effective. Students with sloppy or nuisance behaviors, as well as students who appear lazy, are often floating in abstraction; contracting is a way of grounding them and holding them to their promises.

In one of my favorite stories, "The Scarlet Ibis," by James Hurst, an older brother is in charge of pulling his physically challenged five-year-old brother around in a cart. Owing to frailty and over-coddling by the the boy's mother, little Doodle had never learned to walk. Big brother detested the task of hauling Doodle everywhere; moreover, he was embarrassed at having a brother of school age who couldn't walk. He was determined to teach the little boy to stand first, and then walk. But Doodle's legs were weak, and time after time he'd collapse to the ground. Brother would prop him up again. "I can't do it," he'd say. "I can't." But then Brother would describe to him a gray-haired old man with a Rip Van Winkle beard being pulled around in a coaster wagon by another even older man. This never failed to "motivate" the little boy to try again to raise himself to his feet. Eventually Doodle learned to stand, and then to walk.

You can "prop up" the lazy student with encouragement, humor, and also by projecting, at times, the consequences for not trying hard enough. Where will she be and what will she be doing at 18, 21, or 45? Watching "soaps" doesn't even pay minimum wage yet. Thinking is hard work; what can we do to get the reluctant student to think?

There are several other considerations with regard to labeling a student "lazy." First of all, decide if he or she is learning. I have had students who never even read a story but who, because of superior auditory skills, would pass a test on the topic. Determine, then, if he or she is listening. Does he or she show any signs of recognition or interest? If so, perhaps your real concern is that he or she is failing. It is the child's poor grade in your class that disturbs you.

Parents need to know if their youngster is not earning a decent grade, but *you* are not responsible for a student's poor grades, unless, of course, you are doing a poor job of teaching. The lazy student who is merely failing can be encouraged, but for you to care more about a grade than the child does is pretty silly, don't you think?

What about the lazy student who is not learning? This *is* distressing. Life is going on, leaving this person behind. How will he or she ever catch up? The child has done nothing all quarter. We are beginning fractions next week and he or she can't even do short division! Studies have shown that youngsters who begin school at the age of ten will reach proficiency of their peers by about the age of eleven. Non-English-speaking students who emigrate to our country prove how quickly learning can occur.

Students will learn and perform when they have to.

Now, you *can* attempt to design a curriculum of life or death import if you wish! There *are* such curriculums. The Navy Seals have one, as do skydiving schools, and you can also find life or death training at those orientation sessions for pee-wee soccer officials. Mostly, though, you need to respect the lazy student's right to be lazy and yes, his or her right to fail. Failure may be a goal for this child. You are wrong to invoke alarm and panic. Kids lose respect for us when we try too hard to make them care about what *we* think is important. They become suspicious of our loud groans and gnashing teeth. We seem frenetic and primitive to them and lose all credibility. Don't just simply abandon these kids; treat them like the other kids:

Hi. How ya doin'? How about those Packers? I like your shirt. How was the Ricky Martin concert? Want to pass a test?

In short, lighten up. Not many people make "lazy" a way of life. At some point, there is a trail to follow, a boy or girl ahead of them making tracks, kicking up dust in a mysteriously inviting way.

Slow

I personally cannot think of a better word than *slow* to describe an academically challenged student whom his or her peers would call "dumb." The thesaurus is of no help: *snail-like, pokey, listless, sloth-like.* But most of us know what *slow* means. If I tell a parent, "Jeff sure is a nice kid, but . . ." most of the time he or she is going to fill in the blank with *slow*. The parent knows it takes Jeff longer to do things. He walked late and learned to tie his shoes months later than his older brother did. It takes him longer to do things.

With certain kinds of tasks, he's slow.
Yes, Mrs. Geranium. English is not easy for him.
Never has been. Me, now, I liked English, read everything I could, but his dad . . . didn't do so well in school. Jeff takes after him.

Which is good, because Jeff's dad is a hard worker and good father who takes his boys fishing and hunting and teaches them woodworking, skills incidentally, which Jeff learned very quickly. Every summer and fall, the family takes camping trips. They all like each other. But Jeff is falling farther and farther behind, and in a year or two he may just quit school because he's become angry about feeling dumb. This is a shame, for Jeff is not dumb; he has learned to write and read at a fifth-grade level by the time he's in ninth grade, and with persistence and enough time, will read and write like a ninth grader.

Jeff is a slow learner. *Slow*, however, is another four-letter word. We sometimes spend graduate tuition dollars and whole summers learning euphemisms for *slow*. Even more distressing is that the condition of being a slow learner is given almost no official acknowledgement—an area of neglect that hugely impedes our plans for helping all children succeed. Educators are reluctant to suggest that some students just aren't as quick to learn as others. This denial—often shared equally by parents—torments many of these youngsters, forcing some to develop the kind of antisocial behavior that will eventually qualify them as Emotionally-Behaviorally Disordered (EBD).

Simply put, *slow* deserves some respect, and kids who learn slowly need—and deserve—more attention, especially early on. These children should not have to devolve into lower primates in order to get the individualized help they need. First, though, we have to admit that all children are not intellectually equal. Five to 20 percent of all youngsters in the same age group are far more challenged in learning and several years behind the larger part. They can't negotiate new territory at a pace with the other 80 percent any more than a two-year-old can match a four-year-old in walking without stumbling through a room with toys, balls, and alphabet building blocks strewn across the floor. Yet, rather than risk hurting anyone's feelings, we say that if a child lags behind, then it's the fault of extraneous obstacles in his or her path. This denial has to end, and time and attention must be spent on, and funded for, slow learners. And if that doesn't happen soon, then what?

Do your best to encourage these kids. Reward their efforts and time on task equally with academic performance so that they can pass your class and feel that school is still worthwhile. Discover what they enjoy doing and engage them in conversations about things they do well—football, skateboarding, gardening, baby-sitting, singing, dancing, or telling jokes. Be honest. Explain that they are making progress, but as with painting window trim or peddling a bike, some people naturally move faster than others. Academic learning takes everyone's time. Urge each of these children to accept that it may take a little more of his or hers.

Alphabet Blocks and Inhalers

Often there are mitigating factors in the student conditions of lazy or slow. Picture a young child in a room full of alphabet blocks and toys. At first, he or she will stumble over the toys and the alphabet blocks alike. In time, the child will learn to negotiate these obstacles and even enjoy them. But he or she learns this more quickly if a parent is present to help guide him or her through this difficult course. This ultimately makes teachers' jobs easier. But sometimes parents ignore the lettered blocks and concentrate on moving their kids toward the toys and balls, where stumbling is expected and even applauded as a healthy growth experience. Focusing on the world of games, uniforms, trophies, and inter-city travel and competition is often encouraged by well-meaning adults who think Jimmy's self-esteem needs a boost since he can't read and is failing in school.

Later, these same adults may expect each teacher to modify his or her academic curriculum to allow for time and energy lost to toys and games. Should each of us adapt our educational delivery to cut corners and use our big feet to kick aside basic academic things? If we do, our individualized tutorials invariably become little "Pac" men and women who swallow many of the troublesome—but necessary—alphabet blocks. If Jimmy gets ice time at 5:00 a.m., or if Jenny needs to go to open gym beginning September 1 in order to have a chance at making varsity, then academic practice—for example, homework—becomes the set of alphabet blocks that threaten the amount of time spent with the toys and balls that

"every healthy child needs." Administrators and teachers must have the courage to admit that parents don't always know best when it comes to absenting their kids from instructional time or from home study. I know of one case where a talented ninth grader spent a whole academic quarter attending a golf school in Florida. Teachers at his home school were expected to provide him with assignments and materials for that entire nine weeks, then correct the work and give him a grade. Students immersed in non-academic priorities may appear academically slow or lazy, or may become that way if we agree to do too much for them.

As if other distractions weren't enough, youngsters now face an increasing number of medical issues. Many of the ills of society and the environment have come to rest with the youngest and most vulnerable; fetal alcohol syndrome is a good example. And when you went to school, how many of your classmates carried inhalers? Things have happened in our environments that have eroded the robust American child of the 1950s and 1960s. We may be mystified by why kids seem more fragile today, but we must support and nurture children as they come to us, not as we wish they were.

Yes, schools need more teachers and aides. We need training and time to learn technologies. We need a community of parents with common sense and an objective view of what can reasonably be expected of their children. But even if we get none of these things, we must still teach these children as they are, and in just the way we would want a colleague to teach our own.

Documentation and Accountability

The potential for helping particularly needy students is greatest when you have kept careful documentation or have enlisted a student's help in creating an account of his or her behavior. Be prepared to begin documentation on the first day of school. What these students do and say needs to be recorded from the moment they first catch your attention in some way that caused you to react with a *Hmmm*. You will know soon enough the kids who need special help. The child who interrupts, doesn't respond to correction, intimidates or bullies others, or withdraws needs to be mentioned. The student's behavior must be described with his or her exact words and actions. So must yours. You absolutely *must not be complacent* about documentation. It is a critical tool for correcting student behavior and for protecting yourself from being second-guessed.

Remember that what you document may eventually be read by the student, the parents, the administrators you work for, and even the courts. Your safest and most effective approach is to be *specific* in describing what you see and hear. *Goofing off* or *screwing around*, while anecdotally accurate, are not terms I'd recommend to show what you regard as troublesome or inappropriate. A safer and possibly more effective tactic is to have the student engage in self-documentation.

The cases on pages 33 and 34 are representative of many instances of documentation that I have used with students, their parents, and my school administrators. In the first example, I recorded incidents on a daily basis. I knew that the student was an EBD candidate and wanted my earliest interventions to be noted so that he could be considered for the program as early as possible. The second case is more a summary statement of how the student had operated up to the last few weeks of the quarter. The concerns I had with each student are clear enough in the context of my comments that I won't review the history of each incident.

September 13
SUBJECT: Possible EBD Referral
Student—Allen F.

1. Monday, 9-12. Allen tapped the shoulder of the boy in front of him three times within the first two minutes of receiving the writing assignment. I asked him if he had a question; I'd be happy to help him. He shook his head "no." After the third time, I moved Allen to the front where I thought he would be less distracted by peers and perhaps more willing to ask me for help instead of interrupting a classmate.

2. Tuesday, 9-13. Allen did not have his homework done today, even though I made a special effort to send it with him on Monday.

3. Wednesday, 9-14. Allen asked frequent questions about the task of recopying his essay, even though the instructions had been gone over and were set out before him on a sheet. Allen seems to think everything should happen for him without thought or effort. At least, he seemed to believe I should do the assignment for him. Since he asked for so much of my attention today, I have told Allen he may hereafter ask only two questions a day. I'm hoping he'll be less likely to waste them then on things that have already been explained to him or given to him in writing.

4. 9-14. Allen repeatedly left his seat to join others at the book table, even though he was told to finish his writing first.

5. 9-14. I reminded Allen that he needed to earn daily points in order to pass the class, but that he could also be given a zero, or minus points. A "1" is given when a student uses the class time well and does not interfere with others. I give a "0" if the time was not used well. I give minus points when the student distracts others. Today, Allen would have earned minus points.

6. 9-15. Allen, again, did not have his homework completed. I explained to Allen that teaching is the only thing I do now at school and that I love my job. I'll be happy to work with him any afternoon after 2:30. In the event he is distracted during class time or doesn't get all his questions answered, this would be a good way to do things. Allen said earlier he hoped to improve his grades this year. I reminded him of that. Allen said he enjoys riding his motorcycle after school.

7. 9-16. I asked Allen about the writing assignment that is now overdue. He said he was going to write about his motorcycle, but just hadn't got around to doing it. I sent a note home with him asking his mother if she would like to help him do a proper job. Personally, I don't think a boy should be allowed to ride a motorcycle if he can't do a proper job of writing about it.

8. 9-17. I reminded Allen, again, that I give a daily grade and that he can pass my class by earning the daily point. I have gone over this with Allen twice now and explained any parts he did not understand.

After a second week of documentation and interventions, I recommended Allan for EBD. Though sometimes tedious, this documentation of Allen's behaviors and my response to it proved vital in getting him considered for special help.

The following documentation was actually presented to the student in question, Geoff I. I felt Geoff would benefit from reviewing my formal account, then responding to it contractually.

November 11
SUBJECT: Incomplete Grade
        Student—Geoff I.

Yesterday, Geoff approached me for the second time in two days to show me progress he'd made on his book report. This was prompted by the grade report of a "D-" I'd given him for the quarter. Clearly, Geoff was not happy with that grade and wanted a chance for at least a "C-."

When I give a final grade for the quarter it is rare that I'll allow a student more opportunities to raise that grade. I told him this. Before this final week, I had reminded Geoff on at least three occasions that he'd need a book report to get the grade he wanted. In each case, Geoff ignored my suggestions. Earlier, he had ignored the journal assignment, declaring that he "hates to write." Why he hates to write I don't know, as he is a more-than-adequate writer, very skilled in seeing proper sentence constructions, and often imaginative. In any case, Geoff operated far below his potential for the whole quarter, and too often he did not use class time well. Why I agreed to extend him a chance to raise his grade I don't know. Partly, I think, it was his insightful moments in class discussion—minus some whining and complaining—that suggested Geoff might finally be maturing and taking a positive hand in his own future. In any event, I've given him an incomplete; this will become a "C" in three weeks under the following conditions:

1. That he completes a book report of at least "B" quality.

2. That he be currently up to date—by December 2—on all class assignments, including the following:

   a.) 600 words in his journal

   b.) Seven hours on the Reading/Writing log

   c.) An "A" on daily use of time

   d.) The "Now I'm 35" story

   e.) All spelling and vocabulary lessons

3. Geoff must also have a folder—in good condition—for English, and his two notebooks in the room at all times during class.

4. Geoff must continue his positive and insightful contributions to class discussion.

I've spoken with Geoff about most of these conditions. He agrees that he was very lax the first quarter, and we both know that ignoring my suggestions was a kind of test, an adolescent power move by Geoff. Geoff is very bright, and has since agreed to work hard on all assignments, even those he strongly dislikes. Geoff agrees this would show his continued interest and maturity. I'm looking forward to following his progress through the end of the quarter.

Mr. Mahle

I have read and agree with Mr. Mahle's comments and the contract we discussed for raising my grade.

Geoff I.

At parent conferences a few weeks later, I showed Geoff's parents this document. They had approached me, bristling that their bright son had fared so poorly in English. Before leaving, they admitted that Geoff has historically "seen how little he can do to get by, especially the first quarter."

Frequently, I will ask students to document their own behavior. This then makes them account-able to themselves and to me. I've used the Daily Self-Evaluation form on page 36 with students who need regular reminders about positive behavior goals. Often, I will present it to them with the idea that filling it out each day will earn credit. Kids like to earn credit. Any child who needs this form already knows he or she needs help; most children want to pass. They know that earning credit is helpful in passing a class. Yes—it is that simple.

Sara, you and I both know that you are having a tough time with things in here.

What do you mean?

Well, we talked just yesterday about being on time, bringing your things, and using your time well.

I said I'd bring my stuff today.

Did you bring your pencil and assignment?

I brought a pencil.

I know it's hard to remember everything. And we both want you to do well. You don't really want to take ninth grade English again next year.

No way.

So, what if I let you use a help sheet that other kids who've struggled have found useful? I'll even give you some extra credit for filling it out each day.

What is it?

It's something to remind you of the things you need to do each day in order to succeed and grow more mature. You want to grow more mature and learn to be more responsible, don't you?

I guess.

Take a look and see what you think.

Yeah, OK, I'll look at it.

Name _____ Period _____ Date _____

DAILY SELF-EVALUATION

Please answer all items completely (circle one).

1. I was on time. **YES** **NO**

2. I brought all necessary materials. **YES** **NO**

3. I did not distract others. **I DID NOT** **SORRY, I DID**

4. I followed directions. **YES** **NO**

5. I had a positive attitude. **YES** **NO**

6. I was on task. **ALL THE TIME** **MOST OF THE TIME**

   A LITTLE BIT **NOT AT ALL**

7. State one thing you **LEARNED** today:

   _____

8. State one thing you did to **HELP** your own learning today:

   _____

   _____

9. On a scale of 0 to 5, (5 being outstanding), rate your overall **PERFORMANCE** today:

   _____

Please sign your name here and present the completed form to your teacher when you are dismissed.

   _____

● **TEACHER:** Note any items you don't agree with, or offer relevant comments:

   _____

   _____

   _____

Some teachers have used the Daily Self-Evaluation form as part of a behavioral contract with kids. This is an effective reminder with youngsters. The few students I've used it with answered honestly nearly every day. Some did not change their behavior all that much, but at least I had self-documentation to support my belief that the child needed extra help. The evaluations are also proof that you've attempted a positive intervention on behalf of a troubled child.

On many occasions I have asked students to give written accounts of their behavior. I've not done this to punish—never use writing to punish—but rather, to encourage them to reflect in a way that may produce more mature behavior. Sue was asked to leave class after several warnings about excessive talking. I gave her the following assignment:

Please answer in complete sentences:

What was the reason for your being asked to leave the room?

I think I was asked to leave the room because I was talking and not doing my work. Also because I was asked to be quiet several times.

Why do you feel you should be allowed back into class?

I think I should be allowed back in the class because it's boring out in the hall and because I feel stupid standing out there doing nothing.

How do you intend to prevent having to be asked to leave in the future?

I guess I will try to do my work without talking and disturbing the class so I will not be sent out of the room again.

I don't remember if Sue improved her behavior, but at least she thought about it and took the blame for her dismissal from class. Most students don't want to account for inappropriate behavior; knowing that they will be asked to write about what they've done wrong discourages wrongdoing.

After collecting several tardy slips from me, Lisa was asked to define and explain punctuality in a properly constructed essay of about 150 words:

Punctuality, 'N, Being On Time, Promptness

Punctuality is important to everyday life in many respects. For example, being late to school or a class can cause you to write essays like this. When you get older, and have a full-time job, being late can cause you to be fired or give you a bad job record. If you are the type of person who is constantly late, you earn that social reputation and it's hard to get rid of.

Being late is a very annoying thing to everyone involved. No one likes to wait, and waiting for the same person over and over again is very irritating.

Sometimes being late can cause major problems. Like if you're late to the airport, you'll miss your flight and if you're late to your wedding, you won't get married.

In conclusion, I am terribly sorry if I inconvenienced your class, and I'll try hard to be on time in the future.

Lisa's wise and amusing essay supports the notion that requiring punctuality is one of the most valuable things we can do for kids. I've kept her account all these years in a file with similar examples written by kids, explaining and taking responsibility for a variety of nuisance behaviors.

I've rarely had to share these with a parent or counselor, but when a student would occasionally backslide, I would find his or her earlier confession and ask if he or she recognized the handwriting. This subtle reminder usually proved to be an adequate corrective.

What should you do about late assignments? It's always been wrenching for me to refuse late work or give it no credit. But students must also be held accountable. I decided that I'll take late work for partial credit if I get a note from the child's parent. This then involves parents in the accountability process. (I've made exceptions for students without parents and allowed them to get notes from their counselors instead.)

> Dear Mr. M.,
> I am aware that my daughter, Melinda, is turning her journal in late. Thank you.

> Dear Mr. M.,
> Beth told me she lost her English assignment and that she could only resubmit it if she had a note from me. Please accept Beth's late work.

> Dear Mr. M.,
> Ben really did leave his English essay in Duluth during the hockey tournament this weekend. Please accept his work late for partial credit.

My own accountability sometimes requires writing letters home. In these, I try to emphasize the positive qualities of the student while reiterating or documenting my specific concerns. When I've spoken with a parent, I like to include what he or she has said to me about the child, so the parent can respond if I have misrepresented that conversation. It is my goal to inform the parent of the current concerns I have for his or her child and to enlist the parent's cooperation. I always include a number where I can be reached, and may include a copy of my grading system and classroom expectations.

October 17, 2000

Dear Mr. G,

Thank you for your support during our Monday phone conversation. I think you realize that with the large number of students I have, this letter represents a measure of special interest in your son. Mark is bright, personable, and a class leader—a person well worthy of extra investment. But you know this.

You described Mark as having a tendency to "motor mouth." Yes. But when he shows self-control and maturity, he adds appropriate energy and insight into class discussion. He is also an able writer when he makes the effort. I would project, conservatively, high Cs and Bs in English when Mark really begins to work. For the time being, though, I'll be happy with some strong effort at self-discipline, for I absolutely must have the best learning environment. I insist that Mark contribute to that. To do less would rob many kids of what may be their only chance to complete their English assignments or to get personal help from me.

Mark will argue that he is not the only one who talks at the wrong times. True. He is, however, usually the first, and because of his recognized leadership, several others take their cues from him. We must guide his influence into positive channels. Mark must take his cues from me.

His first cue is this: Mark must avoid any conversation, sign language, lip reading, eye contact, or mental telepathy with Mike T.—and with any of several girls who so admire him—during class readings, discussions, or individual work time.

Finally, I think we need to emphasize to Mark that he has been given some real advantages in life. He's bright, healthy, a talented athlete, well-liked, and enjoys a good home environment. He has a great future. It's time he builds on those strengths by first giving up the distracting behaviors more typical of kids younger then he.

Incidentally, setting aside time for Mark to study on a regular basis would be excellent—Kids always have homework, at least a book to read or a journal in which to explain or complain or celebrate the day. This habit will be invaluable as the year gets tougher and as he goes into tenth grade. Thanks again for your time and support. Feel free to call me anytime after 3 p.m. here at the school.

Sincerely,
MR. BENJ MAHLE, English 9

In the next letter, I approach the subject of drug use as tactfully as I can. I support my mention of this issue by discussing specific behavior.

October 23, 2000

Dear Mr. and Mrs. Z,

This letter is to share my concern for Mike's low achievement in English. Enclosed you will see a copy of the daily grading system I use with ninth graders. I believe it is reasonable to expect that kids this age make good use of class time. Mike has not done well at this in recent weeks. He has not been disruptive, but has, instead, simply not done the work—even though I know he is a capable student when he applies himself.

On several occasions, Mike has slept. Though it is the last hour of school, I very rarely have students fall asleep! I guess I must wonder how much sleep he is getting on weeknights. In my experience, sleeping in class usually indicates kids are being overextended through involvement in sports, jobs, or staying out late with friends. I am also bound to mention that sleeping in class and/or disinterest in school achievement are symptoms of a youth's involvement with chemicals.

Mike is currently five points below passing in his daily work, and I have twice told him that I'd be available to work with him after school. On one occasion, Mike agreed to meet and then did not show up. I know you live some distance from school, yet I have seen Mike on several occasions riding a bike around school grounds well after 3 p.m. I am guessing that Mike can arrange for rides home if he stays beyond the time when buses leave.

I will be happy to listen to any suggestions you might have concerning ways I could motivate your son. I do not threaten kids or harass them beyond reminding them about work that is due. I know Mike is able to choose his behavior. At present, he is choosing to fail. I will continue to encourage him to meet with me for the purpose of getting him into a passing status. I don't really know what more I can do apart from letting you know of my concerns. Again, if you have suggestions or if I can help in some other way, please contact me through the school office or through Mike's counselor.

Sincerely,
MR. BENJ MAHLE, English 9

Accumulating documentation and statements of accountability can look like harassment. You must avoid this appearance by having just cause. Concern for the student's health, academic progress, attitude, or behavior is reason enough for noting what goes on with him or her. Avoid personal commentaries. Focus on the troubling behaviors, but include side comments about the positive behaviors and the potential for doing better. And always express your interest in seeing the student improve and succeed. Interview the student quietly in the presence of the class, but out of earshot. Other students can testify, if necessary, to the reasonable, non-threatening, non-physical approach you used. To greatly expand your base of power and influence, few things offer as much potential as does the objective process of documentation and accountability. (It can be pretty funny, too!)

For many of us, documentation is easier now than ever. I e-mail myself with specific details of the day. The entries are recorded on my message log. Occasionally, I print out copies of my comments just in case some technological tragedy ensues. It's a good system.

Right and Reasonable

We and our students are entitled to dignified treatment in the process of teaching. This assumes a 99 percent correlation between our understanding of what makes for dignified treatment and what others, especially adolescents, understand that to be. We must be fair and aggressive in making sure that everyone in the fantail of our influence is treated with dignity.

What does this mean in terms of actual teacher behavior? Partly, that students who need reminders about what is appropriate are given clues without sarcasm or disdain:

Excuse me, Judy, but I can't concentrate on Fred's oral report if you are going to talk to Alicia. Could your conversation wait until after class?

We must try not to embarrass kids for being temporarily wrong. When possible, we give them the chance to adjust and save face before we intervene. We offer to discuss differences of opinion privately. And most of all, we listen. Often we contract with kids in ways that allow their input:

So, what can you suggest we do to help you avoid talking with Alicia when you need to be silent?
Ah, you could take off points.
Will that help you get a better grade in here?
Hmmm. No.
Any other ideas?

I guess you could move us . . . if it happens again.
You agree, then, that you and Alicia should be separated if you talk to each other when you shouldn't?
Yes, if we can have another chance.
Can you explain this to her so she knows what your plan of improvement is?
Sure.

- Accept kids as imperfect.

- Remember, too, that flashes of temper may not require as harsh a consequence as behavior that has been premeditated.

- Show students that you are their ally by ensuring that their views are heard as quickly as possible.

- Give second chances while making the conditions under which those chances are offered as clear and simple as possible.

- Avoid power struggles.

- Swallow your urge to be clever—Few kids can spar with us verbally. Remember that even an unpopular child who gains your attention by misbehaving is likely to have peers who are quietly on his or her side.

- Finally, accept that the modeling and reviewing of appropriate behavior is as much a part of teaching as are multiplication tables, constitutional amendments, osmosis, or parts of speech.

Reason rules. On rare occasions, though, it is right not to push reasoning with a child who simply won't give you the chance. When a student is intractable, you must pass responsibility for that person to a higher authority. Where the right of the class to learn is threatened, promptly move disruptive students to a time-out area of the classroom. Be prepared for this at all times by having the office phone number memorized. If you have no phone, designate a student in each class to run urgent messages from you to the office.

Know the people in your school who can assist you. These may be counselors, teacher aides, or administrators. Speak regularly with these people to gain assurance that if worse comes to worse, one or more of them can assist you at a moment's notice.

Some youngsters must eventually be removed from your building or even from the community where you are teaching. You are not responsible for seeing that this happens; you must simply protect your turf and realize that a few students will never get what they need from you, and that not all students can be taught successfully in your school setting.

This is an especially hard fact for young teachers to accept. We begin our careers with vigor and idealism, ready to go the extra ten miles. This is right, and many students succeed because of our dedication. Some students love us for this . . . and then one day we meet Lenny.

Lenny would like to love you, but he hurts too much. He wants to hurt someone, and you are available and easy to get to. You try compassion and encouragement; you take a moment each day to ask him how he's doing; you give him little jobs around the room to show you trust him and believe in his capabilities. You give him chalk and

the quote of the week to print on the board and then find, along with the quotation, a stick figure with a big head, hair styled a lot like yours, and a long stick-finger stuck up one large nostril.

That's funny. The kids think so, and you show what a sport you are by telling Lenny that you think he's parted your hair on the wrong side. This is about all you can do to show Lenny how you flex and bend. You ask him to erase the figure, because after the laugh, it can only be a distraction—and besides, you don't want to keep answering questions from your other classes about how they might hire the artist to show them how to draw so well.

There. You've shown you can take some kidding. Lenny hasn't completely fallen from grace. But you notice that he seems perturbed that the class is lending you support for your big view of the incident, chuckling at your remarks. Lenny refuses to erase the caricature, so you do it for him. No big deal.

Later, Lenny begins making animal noises; the other kids are annoyed. You ignore it, but it continues. After class, you arrange a private meeting with Lenny. You listen, offer him a chance to correct himself, give suggestions when he expresses confusion, and ask him if others are being treated fairly when he disrupts.

But you cannot reach Lenny. His disruptions continue, and when you hear him raking the girl next to him with sexually inappropriate comments, you know he has to go. Fortunately, you have documented all his behaviors and your responses since the first time, days ago, that Lenny caught your attention. You've called his parents, spoken with his counselor, and referred him to your principal. Nothing has changed his behavior and your teaching is suffering. The class is falling behind, and Lenny is the cause. You may even admit to yourself that you don't like Lenny so well anymore.

All this is OK. And so you tell your principal (and counselor perhaps) that Lenny can no longer be a part of your class. You will continue to offer assignments, of course, but Lenny is wrecking the opportunities of others, and he must go. This is right and reasonable.

It is common sense to excise a thorn from under your fingernail. You can't concentrate on your work or on any phase of your life with a thorn working its way into the sheltered pink skin under the brim of your nail. Of course, there are parents and colleagues who will say that permitting the thorn under your nail is a part of your job—but they are wrong. That thorns occasionally find a fleshy part of you is a risk of teaching. But insisting that any of us allow it to remain, to inflame and infect us, is sadistic. Our misery will infect those around us. We have a responsibility to remove such a thorn.

Still, ideas of supreme self-sacrifice are most often perpetuated by ourselves and have as their basis the miracle worker myth: *The belief that we can save all kids.* We can't. I do insist that we try for a while. But we should never ignore the safety and the rights of the 30 other students in our care. We should never ignore threats to our physical or mental health.

Use your common sense. Hopefully, the expectations your school has for students will help you. Learn them before you spend a single day in the classroom; ask about them even as you interview for a job. Know, too, that policy may be little more than theory in some schools. Check with teachers and aides in your building to learn how well you can expect to be supported. This knowl-edge will help determine how easily you can go about making your room right.

But regardless of building policies or the enforcement you see, be prepared to stand strong.

Ninety-nine percent of the world's people will agree that civility supercedes a child's right to display creative misbehavior. This huge majority expects you to encourage high standards of student achievement and behavior. Remember that the number of children who truly cannot control what they do is far less than you are led to believe. Remember that on those rare occasions when you've been reasonable and still not managed to get a student on track, it is OK to provide some quiet time-out. Never be intimidated away from doing what you know is reasonable and right.

10 THINGS

I've Learned the Hard Way

1. Fairness and justice are not the same. Kids don't want fairness, where everyone is treated the same, where they have to share their sandwiches with the kids who forgot theirs. They want justice, where each person is treated accordingly with respect to the particular circumstances. Never promise to be fair, but make every effort to be just.

2. Raising your voice is largely ineffective.

3. Give kids the benefit of the doubt.

4. Always be prepared, but don't feel obliged to defend what you do.

5. Remember that you are teaching kids, not just subject matter. You may be wise to keep this to yourself.

6. Work within the curriculum until you are sure enough of your clientele, the community, the administration, and yourself to introduce potentially controversial new material.

7. Do not teach mediocre material just to make a point.

8. You will not sensitize all students.

9. Encouraging students to think is a noble aspiration that will be met with constant resistance. Good writing, for instance, requires thought; that's why school is sometimes hard work.

10. Don't correct everything.

Lunchroom Duty: My Dialogue with Bryan

Teachers are sometimes reluctant to perform tasks outside of the classroom; they don't see these duties as "real teaching." Actually, these settings offer us opportunities for doing some of our *best* teaching.

The lunchroom is a place where students expect you to be at your worst. Lunchrooms traditionally are noisy with the chatter of happy kids. Kids are happy to be eating with their friends. We should not fret over noise in the lunchroom unless it interferes with what kids are most entitled to do joyfully—eat and talk. This sometimes means addressing the negative behavior of kids who either have no friends or no food.

Bryan was a boy with no friends. To get attention, he began tapping the top of his lunch table boisterously. He was a powerful youngster, and his drumming created a thunderous sound that often surprised kids in mid-swallow. This caused numerous guttural choking sounds and chocolate milk to spew from the noses of startled students. My first day in the lunchroom, I approached Bryan about his drumming:

Bryan, several people have complained that you pound the lunch table day after day. With 300 kids in here, there is always some noise, but even so, your pounding rises above all of that. After your first outburst I noticed Ms. Adams talking with you. Did she ask you to stop?

It wasn't me, it was . . .

You were pounding the table. I saw it. Did she ask you to stop?

Yes.

Did you stop?

No.

Bryan, you've probably noticed that we have teaching assistants who help the mentally handicapped kids eat.

The retards? I don't look at 'em. They're gross!

The assistants are instructed to remove those kids if they throw food or pound the table. Do you think you should be expected to behave at least as well as the kids who are severely handicapped and have to be helped to eat?

Pausing, thinking.

Ahhh. Yeah, I guess.

That would mean you do not pound on the table. Will you agree to stop pounding tables at lunch?

Yes.

Good. Keeping your word means you won't need special help to control yourself, and you can stay at lunch with the rest of us. Does that seem like a good plan?

Yes.

Great. I'll write up a little something to show that we had this little talk and that you've decided to take responsibility for yourself. Nice going, Bryan. See you tomorrow.

Yeah. See ya.

Bryan is large for an eighth grader, over six feet tall and about 200 pounds, and known for bullying other kids. He is in the EBD class at our school and is therefore familiar with contracting and documentation. I wanted proof of this intervention, proof that I'd been reasonable and that Bryan had understood our conversation and had committed himself to behave appropriately. I typed the dialogue as you have just seen it. The next day at lunch, I called Bryan over:

What now? I wasn't pounding tables.

I'm really pleased with that, Bryan. You've kept your word and I want to keep mine now. I've written a record of our conversation yesterday, and I want you to read it to see if I've made any mistakes. Sometimes my memory isn't so good at my age, you know.

(Bryan reads my account of the intervention.)

Yeah, OK.
Great. Would you sign this then?
Why?

I figure you'll be famous someday, and your autograph will be worth a lot of money.

Yeah, right.

Actually it's more important than that. Your signature will show that we have been clear and honest about what we discussed, and that I didn't make up the good part where you agree to take care of yourself. Your signature now is important because when a man signs his name to something, it means he plans to keep his word. Will you sign?

Where?

On that line at the bottom, right after where it says, "This signature confirms that Bryan and I discussed this issue in the manner that is shown above."

There's two lines.
I sign the other one.
I get it.

Bryan signed. I had documentation, and Bryan had backed up his "good word" with his "good name." Now we'll see if he backs that up with good behavior. Thereafter, Bryan did avoid pounding on tables.

I was able to confront Bryan on other occasions, including one time in the hallway when I hollered, "Hey, man!" just as he was about to clobber a pesty seventh grader who had underestimated Bryan's tolerance for being teased about his big feet. I believe that because of our previous agreement, "Hey, man" meant something then, when it really counted. Young boys like Bryan who have exceptional size are often expected to be better behaved than smaller children—to be more mature. Usually they are. I think addressing them as men implies a greater expectation and urges cooperation.

Contracting, too, is an adult form of compromise and promise. To complete a contract, Bryan needed to sign his name. This reminded him that he had power over the implementation of the plan and over his behavior as well. Any student who can be made to see that he or she can gain something by changing a behavior can be contracted with.

Though this kind of procedure takes time, it is well worth it when a student has a history of broken promises. It documents your interest in helping the child to change for the better. It can be used as a reminder to the child of his or her willingness to make changes for the better, or it can give proof of a promise kept. It's a great way to talk with kids, as well as an impressive intervention in the eyes of parents and administrators.

Being Back

Ten years ago, I took a year-long sabbatical. Upon returning, the first entry in my school journal for 1988–89 began this way:

6 September, 1988 2:53 p.m.

My back is sore, my feet ache, my voice is wavering and thin. I have survived this day through the grace of God.

After first period, I was afraid my voice wouldn't carry me through this opening day of school. I had a lot to say and couldn't count on getting from these kids the attention I'd been used to in other years. Even though I've taught 16 years here, after being gone a year on sabbatical leave, I had no reputation to assist me. The kids in this room were seventh graders when I left; they didn't know me then, and from the get-go it was obvious they couldn't have cared less about who I am now. Honestly, I've never felt so panicked in the classroom.

My class behaved like jerks beginning with our homeroom period. They booed the principal when he came on over the closed circuit with his "Welcome back to school" spiel. It didn't help that his cue cards were too high and made him appear to be looking over the viewers' heads as he spoke. Moreover, the room television, mounted high in the corner, emphasized his misdirection.

Even louder groans greeted the vice principal as she offered her warm greetings, then reviewed the behavioral expectations for the school. They scoffed when she mentioned "mutual respect," "appropriate language," and "punctuality." They guffawed at "civilized lunchroom behavior" and keeping the newly painted school clean. I thought, "Should I intercede at this point and scold them for their insolence? Discuss citizenship?"

The belligerent, negative attitudes of these kids on the first day caught me off-guard and made me afraid.

What had happened here in the last year? These kids had little respect for our administrators and even less for me, obviously, since they felt so free to ridicule my colleagues right in front of me. It was almost as though I were not present!

The expectations were clear and reasonable. What was going on?

Did these kids think a school should operate like the street? I knew I'd have to address this, and soon. I couldn't ignore this mood of resentment. But if I jumped in too quickly, I would sound like the voices they were mocking. And yet, the students didn't have any sense of what was important if we were all to stay sane and learn!

Their insensitivity continued even when a fellow student appeared on the screen and read the announcements of fall sports activities. This reaction to something as benign as the morning announcements? What can I expect when we read aloud the love poetry of *Romeo and Juliet*?

Halfway through the broadcast, still amazed by the negative banter of my homeroom, I turned my focus to the television screen. I began listening, listing facts, perhaps thinking in my purely academic mindset, that I ought to review with these insolent kids the things they must know.

I realize, now, that I also needed to tune them out; to listen to them any more would make it hard to like them.

Ironically, in my year away, I'd written *Power Teaching*, a book of strategies for just these kinds of situations. Now it seemed like I didn't know anything about managing kids. What would I do in this case?

I couldn't wonder for long. I followed my own advice: *Be active. Don't wring your hands. Do something.*

I took notes. The broadcast ended with the school motto: *Build yourself a good day.*

The kids continued to chatter and cackle. I turned off the television and slipped behind my lectern at the front of the room. I gripped the sides hard, pushed myself away, leaning slightly back, straightening and stiffening my arms like I'd seen coaches do at pep rallies, and former alumni who have lettered at a university and been invited back to address a graduating class. I think it's called "pulling yourself up to your full height." From that vantage point I watched the students buzzing in twos and threes. I breathed in a long, slow draught, expanding my chest (and my resolve) before exhaling slowly, trying to expel my tension.

They began to quiet, anticipating something from me. Still, it was not a reaction that I'd ever seen on a first day, when even the most irritating and bold kids are usually quietly studying the "enemy."

Take out a half sheet of paper.
Huh? What? A test on the first day?
Number to ten. . . .

The students were suddenly silent, scrambling for materials and then numbering their papers. How interesting that we've conditioned them so completely to regard tests with this abject seriousness! At another time and place in my career I might have been skeptical about such robotic obedience, but on this day, it was a welcomed ally. (It has remained proudly in my arsenal.)

Of course they'd been testing me too, and I had already sweat through the armpits of my cotton undershirt. In the early moments of their rudeness and mockery I was simply too amazed to conceive a coping strategy. Minutes later, I had a plan. But I really think it was not so much drawn from my repertoire of junior high school experience as primordial memories or instincts basic to survival.

Knowledge or instinct? To last for a career we need both, in any case.

Number one: State the motto for our junior high for this school year.

Two: As best as you can, write word for word the first behavioral expectation told to you by our vice principal.

Number three: . . .

Number ten: Who was announced as the coach this year for your 9th-grade girl's volleyball program?

And finally, in case you may have missed one of the first ten, you can redeem yourself somewhat by giving a thoughtful response to this special bonus question: the word appropriate *was used several times by the vice principal, and it will be used by me. Explain your definition of the word "appropriate."*

Now, correct your own papers. . . .

Those questions were the answer *Listening Quiz Saves Veteran Teacher's Classroom Comeback.* I thank God and any other cosmic force that may have assisted. After 15 months, I truly was back.

Teaching is both a matter of careful planning and eternal vigilance.

Getting the Point

In *Power Teaching*, I recommended using a Daily Point System. Now I'm recommending the *new and improved* Daily Point System. The old version was the most effective and simple measure I've ever found for keeping a class productive and out of trouble; the new system does this with more flexibility and less contemplation.

It works like this: Each period I give each student a daily point (or none) based exclusively on how he or she has used class time—a single point for working the whole period on class assignments. This point is referred to as the T.O.T. for "time on-task." Over the quarter, this translates to 40 or 45 total points and about 30 percent of a student's grade. I distribute a sheet on grading and go over it on the first day of school:

Using class time well will ensure each of you a passing grade. I award 40 to 45 daily points per quarter according to how you use your time in class. To earn the point, you must be working on English the entire period. This will be your job each day. I have never had a student fail who earned all the daily points in a quarter. . . .

Listed below are the activities and possible points for this quarter; you will see that daily points make up nearly 30 percent of your grade.

By staying on task, you are going to succeed in this class, just like you would with any other job. Please ask questions if you don't understand.

A typical student question:

What if we finish our assignments early; can we talk with friends?

Great question! Now here's how it is: You'll need to spend enough time on each assignment to be sure it's done the best way you know how. There is no reward simply for finishing something fast. Learning in here is not a race. Talking to friends is important, sure; but if you finish something ahead of your classmates you'll be expected to do any of several other things, such as journal writing or reading a library book. Otherwise, you may mess up your friends' work, you know? Like if they see you're done and they'd like to talk to you too, and so they kind of blow off the rest of their assignment because they know you're waiting on them? So . . . you're never done in here. I mean, we've got a lot to learn yet before we become the best communicators, readers, thinkers, and writers that we can be.

I have a lot of faith in ninth graders, and so I expect a lot from them too. I know each of you understands how important it is to make good use of time, so I'm going to reward you for that every day.

Teachers need to expedite the grading process whenever possible and use additional time and energy for teaching things like indefinite pronouns or photosynthesis. A point awarded for time on-task is not a "behavioral point." Some parents and administrators will criticize you for a grading system that intentionally or casually forces grades downward for misbehavior, poor attitudes, or shyness. Time on-task is, of course, a behavior. But, it falls into the "effort" category and is therefore widely lauded, especially by parents whose kids find that purely academic Ds or Cs become Cs or Bs with help from the daily point.

A daily point based on time on-task encourages and rewards a work ethic. Kids of every ability level benefit from establishing good work habits. The system is equally effective for slow learners and the gifted since it rewards the principle of practical and mature time management —something that is not inborn in students no matter how bright they are. *It should be obvious— but I will emphasize, too—that a class where everyone is on-task the entire period is a class that learns a great deal more.*

My first deployment of the Daily Point System was intended to modify the behavior of several very bright girls who were finishing work early in my class and then gossiping about and mocking slower students. Once the system was in place, these girls regularly spent time reading in order not to lose credit each period for being off-task. Because the system is simple, reasonable, and equitable for all students, students and their parents see the daily point as a fair reward for daily work.

That's all well and good, but doesn't such a system give a misleading view of what kids are actually learning? Won't the grades be inflated?

I don't worry about inflating grades; not everyone will earn an A. Tests, and especially written work, will separate the As from the Bs and the Bs from the Cs. Yes, I have very few Ds and certainly far fewer failures than in other plans in which grades were earned only by the quality and quantity of finished work. The T.O.T. point is, for most kids, a positive daily reminder of their individual worth. Why not reward and respect effort, especially when students feel recognized and productive because of it? These kids do learn more. Is that not more important than ensuring that their grades reflect an accurate comparison of their academic achievement with that of each classmate? If you answer *No*, welcome to the bell curve.

What about students who are absent?

Students who are absent can't earn the daily point. This discourages truancy and, of course, hurts students who have genuinely good reasons for being gone. For these students, have available make-up work and extra assignments that they can do to recover the lost credit.

I give 500 points a quarter; a daily point won't mean that much in my class.

Make it five daily points then. Better yet, revise your point system downward so that a single point means something. Take all your assignments and divide their point values by five. Or, if a test has 50 items, don't use the word *points*. Instead, refer to it as a *"50-item" test*. Curve the scores to letter grades, and then assign the letter grades a point value. Kids like seeing a letter grade and a point value. An "A" (score of 48–50) could be worth ten points; an A- (a score of, say, 46–47) = 9.5; a B+ = 9; a B = 8.5 ; and so on. I've found that grading assignments requires far less effort with a lower point system. You needn't study and judge each item on a ten-question worksheet and try to decide on a point award of zero to ten. Simply give a completed worksheet two points, a partially finished assignment one, and so on. Under this system you can tally points at the end of the quarter without the help of a calculator.

Do kids really care about the daily point?

Yes! Especially if you make them aware early on of how it affects their grades. Now, a little story.

In my first year with the Daily Point System, I did not have any extremely unruly classes, but I still felt the system helped. I decided I'd use it again. The next year, the system was tested when I encountered the eighth-grade class from hell. Of those 28 students, I later learned that 20 had serious learning or emotional problems. The first day, I explained my grading system. They were polite but restless, and I could see eyes wandering toward the cloud banks just visible outside my south-facing windows. I could see some counting the dots in the ceiling tiles and others checking the corners of the room for spiders and puppies. They were either disinterested or wary. When an "out-of-seat" activity produced some jostling and mean-spirited comments, I knew that kids' histories were colliding in this room. This class would need riveting structure.

The next day, I began conditioning them to sit up straight when the bell rang. Those not in desks at the bell were considered tardy and required to spend a "memory minute" with me at the end of the hour—which, happily, was also the end of the school day. I complimented good posture and never raised my voice, but before the bell sound quit resonating I had already placed a worksheet on the first desk. I walked between rows, handing the assignment to each child—a direct link from me to each of them, not from the student sitting in front who merely passes something on.

The entire first week, I provided the class with a variety of at-the-desk tasks, carefully chosen for student interest and fun (such as crossword puzzles with vocabulary words, or finish-the-story creative writing assignments). I applauded their attention to task and self-control, and at the week's end, gave them a grade.

On-task points were separated from the written assignments and then added together so kids could see how important the daily points had been. I deliberately made the curve very tight: As—10; Bs—8–9; Cs—7; Ds—6.

Example: Fred—T.O.T. = 4 of 5 points. Written work = 3 of 5. Total = 7 of 10. Grade: C.

The students were shocked. Few of them had even remembered what I'd said about "daily points" and "time on-task." But most had done what I'd asked, and when I held up the clipboard with all the ones in rows next to their names, there were murmurs of approval from many of these kids. Most had done poorly in past English classes, but this week had worked hard and had, by this first report, earned five daily points. Several proud students whooped, "I got a B!" It's true that these grades did not reflect student progress in the traditional academic sense. But in the sense of doing what would in the long run benefit the student most, they represented a great deal. These students were rewarded for working, just like in the real world. Eventually their stick-to-itiveness was rewarded even further because of the resulting improvement in the quality of their work—quality encouraged and made possible by eliminating "spare time" that had previously distracted them from doing their best on the tasks at hand. I was able to ease away from the hard structure and engage them in small group work—for brief periods—and even some independent research and oral reports. But the class never complained about structure, for it meant most of them would earn the daily point.

With T.O.T. points, quality of work often improves as students realize there is no advantage to rushing through an assignment; there is no temptation to finish quickly and chat with Jake or Jean. Chatting is not an accredited option.

To encourage maximum self-control and effort, kids need to know that T.O.T. points will be at *least* 25 percent of their grades.

At this point, you may be wondering, "How do I keep track of the Daily Point System?"

I keep a clipboard with standard-sized graph paper on it. The students' names run vertically on the left edge, and columns of little crossword puzzle boxes run left-to-right. There is a space, then, for each student, for each day. In these spaces I record absences, tardies, the T.O.T. point, and a single mark in red each time a student offers an appropriate oral response such as answering or asking a question, or volunteering to read. (The red marks add up to participation points, another component of the total grade.)

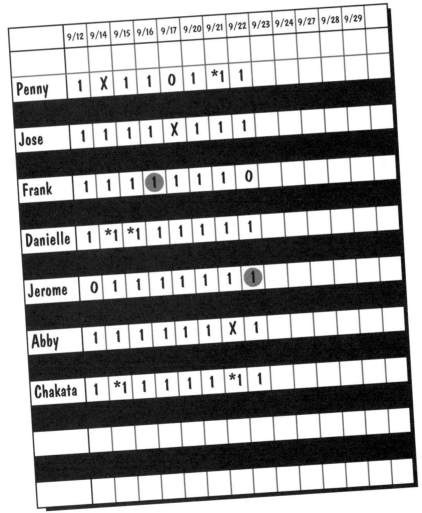

	9/12	9/14	9/15	9/16	9/17	9/20	9/21	9/22	9/23	9/24	9/27	9/28	9/29
Penny	1	X	1	1	0	1	*1	1					
Jose	1	1	1	1	X	1	1	1					
Frank	1	1	1	(1)	1	1	1	0					
Danielle	1	*1	*1	1	1	1	1	1					
Jerome	0	1	1	1	1	1	1	(1)					
Abby	1	1	1	1	1	1	X	1					
Chakata	1	*1	1	1	1	1	*1	1					

It is easy to remember who is on task, because almost everyone is, every day. Participation is also easy to record because I keep the clipboard in front of me during discussions. As kids see me record a mark each time one of them offers an answer, they are encouraged to participate. I always leave the clipboard lying around where students can check to see how they're doing!

Look! I've gotten every daily point this quarter.

That's great, Fred. That's a big reason why you're passing my class.

I mark daily points during the last minute of class. If, during the hour, a student wanders off-task for a minute, I'll go over and quietly offer a reminder:

Janet, how am I going to give you your daily point if you don't find some English to work on?

Or, if it's several students:

Well, now, we still have 25 minutes left in the hour—just time for you guys to earn your points, if you get on-task before the red hand (the second hand on our clocks) hits the 12.

Sometimes kids don't earn the point. Then, at the end of the hour or at the beginning of the next day:

Jake, you took a zero today/yesterday. I reminded you several times about being away from your work here. Is there something more I need to do to make sure you don't string together several zeroes?

Naaah. I'll do good today.

That's such a smart idea, because you can't survive without the daily point, you know? And I really want for you to pass.

Yeah. Me too.

The Daily Point Chart also provides excellent documentation at any meeting in which student progress is discussed. And at parent conferences, it clearly responds to every parent who says something like this:

Sure I'm glad Jack got a B, but how's his behavior?

Have you ever had a parent who wasn't thrilled when you could prove that Jane or Junior was working hard every day in your class? Any time you're asked to show why a student is or is not succeeding, the T.O.T. record provides a convincing testimonial.

The chart has other uses too. In the space at the top or bottom of each daily column, you can note the tasks for that day and know at a glance what the absent student has missed. You can also see which activities encouraged the most participation and those which most challenged your students to stay on-task. But remember, if you plan to give T.O.T. credit, it's crucial that you have standing assignments for students that they can *never finish*, such as free-choice reading or vocabulary. Teachers in any subject area can design such activities, though many schools have adopted the sound philosophy that kids should read any time they're finished with other tasks.

Assigning and charting daily points is not difficult. More importantly, this system shows every student and every interested parent or administrator that you care enough about kids to look at each one individually, every single day.

But It's Just Down the Hall . . .

I stopped giving locker passes this year.

If it's vital that a student have something from his or her locker, he or she will remember it. If it becomes vital sometime during the hour, and the student knows you don't give locker passes, you'll be asked for a bathroom pass. I've found this is rare, however, and concluded that kids don't often really need to go their lockers, as the following ploys indicate.

Come on, Mr. Mahle, it won't take me a second.

I'm sorry, Colleen. I don't give locker passes. You can borrow a pencil and a piece of paper from me.

Mr. Mahle, I forgot it was reading day; my locker's just one floor down.

I'm sorry, Paul. Maybe you can write in your journal or do some vocabulary, or I have books here you might like; but I don't give locker passes. Sorry.

I left my worksheet in my locker and I had it all done!

Gee, I'll bet that makes you mad, eh Cherise? Well, you just bring it in after class, and you can work on something else for now?

Will I lose credit?

Not if it's done and you bring it in right after class.

Can I go to my locker? I need to get something.

I'm sorry. I don't give locker passes. Was it terribly important?

Yes! Yes it was! I'll like die if I don't get this.

What is it? Maybe I have an extra in the room—

Ahhhhh. I don't think so. Oh Mr. Mahle, Pleeeaaaase?

I'm sorry. I don't give locker passes, remember?

Uhmmmmmmm . . . Can I go to the bathroom?

I give bathroom passes as a humanitarian gesture, and because I don't want students to be sick all over my classroom floor. Denying locker passes, however, has been one of the easiest things I've ever done. Kids become more responsible, and I don't have the guilty feeling of introducing kids into the halls during class periods where they can indulge in nuisance behaviors and make noise. For years I'd caved in to pathetic pleas to retrieve a special pen, book, worksheet, a school picture signed just for Bobbi who I'm only in this class with . . . . For years I'd allowed students to not be responsible for bringing all necessary materials to class.

Well, nobody's perfect. Anyhow, that's all over now. I don't give locker passes.

Subs

Dear Mr./Mrs./Ms._____,

Thank you for the privilege of watching over your classes today. The instructions you left were precise and kept the students on-task without any problems. The children were marvelous, as always. You do such a wonderful job of inspiring these children. I've corrected the 150 themes you assigned and entered the grades in your grade book. Thank you again for having me substitute for you. It was a privilege.

Sincerely,

Mrs. Sanford Kelly

Mrs. Kelly was in our building as much as the regular staff. Everyone wanted her to substitute teach when they were going to be gone, and with a regular staff of about 70 teachers, "Kelly" was kept plenty busy.

A retired teacher for some 20 years, Kelly was in her 80s, with limited mobility due to a badly arthritic ankle. It pained us to watch her climb the stairs and then list to one side as she walked down the hallway to "her" room. But she was the best. No day was too dreary, no student too difficult that she couldn't put a positive spin on her experience at the end of the day. Notes like the one above appeared on the top of every teacher's desk, just beneath the tests or essays she'd stayed to correct. At the end of the year, she'd bring treats, thanking us again, "the best staff in the whole school district."

Subs like Mrs. Kelly are rare. She celebrated every teaching day in someone else's room, pretending it was her own. She was strict, but kind. Kids respected her. She knew a great many things and told stories. She left clear notes about what students accomplished, who talked back, or who was late. Mrs. Kelly demanded accountability from kids. This chapter is not intended to tell you how to substitute teach as effectively as Mrs. Kelly. Instead, it will propose one thing with regard to substitute teachers you may have in your room—Design the day in a way that will make each and every student accountable.

Accountability. This begins with the obvious —a seating chart and list of classroom policies. Next, your lesson design must be such that students require little actual teaching of your subject, since the person subbing for your math class may actually be an English major or physical education teacher. Most importantly, however, is that each student should feel that he or she is being observed and monitored by you during the time you are absent. To that end, consider using the form on page 59. I ask my substitutes to give one to each student as soon as the period begins.

Name _____ Period _____ Date _____

SELF-EVALUATION CHECKLIST

This checklist is worth 5 points. Circle one response:

1. I was on time and sat in my assigned place.	**YES**	**NO**
2. I did not ask for passes.	**I DID NOT**	**I DID**
3. I did not distract others.	**I DID NOT**	**I DID**
4. I stayed on-task the whole period.	**I DID**	**I DID NOT**

Listed below are the **ASSIGNMENTS** I was expected to complete during the hour.

I have put a check by those I did complete.

☐ _____

☐ _____

☐ _____

☐ _____

☐ _____

☐ _____

If you answered the questions above positively, you will get **5 POINTS**.

If your teacher does not agree with your evaluation, you will **MEET WITH ME** when I return.

Worksheets will be collected at the end of the period. Lost sheets earn 0 points.

If I know in advance that I'm going to be gone, I give the Self-Evaluation Checklist to my students the day before and review the contents with them, along with the list of assignments to be completed.

I have no tolerance for the mistreatment of substitute teachers. I believe that all schools should have a mandatory out-of-school suspension for students who are insubordinate with a sub. Students who are sent from the room while a sub is in charge are not allowed back in when I return until they think long and hard about their behavior. Before they come back to class, they are required to turn in reflective responses such as the letters below.

There are some very poor substitute teachers

Dear Mr. G.

I sincerely apologize for my behavior in English. I was rude and totally out-of-line.

Please accept my apology. I realize how hard it is to substitute or fill in for a teacher.

In the future I will treat you with respect and as a guest.

Sincerely,

T.B.

Dear Mr. Mahle,

When there's a substitute in my English class I'm expected to act appropriately, and treat this teacher as a guest to the building with respect. I'm to abide by the rules you set down for the class. I'm not to be rude or insubordinate or act inappropriately in any way. It is a privilege to our class to have a substitute and I should recognize this.

Sincerely,

T. B.

working today. However, my feeling is that a healthy school will treat the poor, inadequate, and excellent alike, and that students should be expected to adjust to temporary teachers and treat them with respect. Substitute teachers will spread the fame or shame of your building in many directions—to the community, other schools in your district, and schools in other districts as well.

Finally, if you are in a position to design school policy, the best way to provide substitutes for absent teachers is to enlist the regular teachers in the building to fill in during their free hours by offering comp time or additional pay. Using regular staff discourages kids from taking liberties that they'd be tempted to take with an unknown. It also allows staff to view teaching from the perspective of someone who may teach a different subject, and, in some cases, to work with students who function at varying academic and social levels.

Conferences

*S*o, *are you ready for the longest night of your life? Whoever decided we should have parent/teacher conferences from 3:30 to 9 p.m. after teaching all day must have had a screw loose.*

It wouldn't be so bad, but the parents you really need to see never come!

And those who do only want you tell them how great their kid is . . . .

So what's wrong with that? One of my greatest rewards as a parent was hearing from teachers that I had great kids. One of my greatest joys as a teacher is telling other parents how much I enjoy having Miguel, Marie, Tina, or Sam in my class.

She brightens the room when she walks in. . . .

Sam seems pretty low-key, but he sees things that aren't obvious to other kids, and then in his shy low tone of voice, he cuts to the heart of the matter. I love watching him blush when I repeat his insights to the group.

Many things you share with parents can help them feel that they've been successful with their children. Parenting is the hardest job in the world, and the job which is most devastating to feel you have failed at. Yet the assurances we give parents are only part of the huge value that attends our giving of time to meet with them.

Conferences are also a time when your efforts are acknowledged and praised, and you enjoy the exhilaration of knowing you've made a difference.

If you aren't getting that from conferences, perhaps you've been doing something wrong. And it's not true that parents who most need to come do not. Every parent you see needs to be there, but some need to more than others.

It's nice to meet you, Mrs. Jensen. Briana has really had a tough go of it this quarter.

I was remembering that Briana had taken an "incomplete" after missing the last six days of the term with pneumonia.

It's been terrible. This is her worst report card ever. And the clinic says not to push her, that it could be a year before she gets over this.

Good grief—what kind of pneumonia—

Oh, I'm sorry. I thought you knew, that maybe Briana had written about it in her journal. . . . Her eight-month-old sister died last summer while in her care. She blames herself, of course, constantly—tells me "Mom, I've taken your baby away." She's even talked about having one to replace her sister.

I'm sorry. I didn't know.

I should have told her teachers. So the clinic says to be patient; but I can't wait a year to get her back on track. She knows I don't blame her, and I've told her how I've had to go on, to do my work so that we have food on the table. Am I really not supposed to push her? How is failing her classes going to make her feel any better?

We need a plan. . . .

I had spoken earlier to a colleague about Briana, about how smart she was, but how her absentmindedness and distractibility made her the subject of "dumb blonde" jokes. Now, I knew Briana would need help in defending herself, and that I could make her a "project"—a term I use for kids with special needs whom I feel might be helped through some collaboration with other teachers. I decided to approach Briana's history teacher and, together, devise a strategy for nurturing her through this sad time. Without conferences, we'd have known nothing of Briana's agony and probably would have criticized her quietly for sinking into laziness and apathy. It is best, safest, and most professional to assume that anyone attending a conference needs to be there.

They're Not All on Drugs, But ...

In his journal, Mike admitted that he enjoyed the attention he drew from teachers and administrators concerned about his chemical use. Because his behavior was frequently antisocial, and he did absolutely no schoolwork, and because his hair fell over his shoulders, drug use was suspected.

They get me down at the chemical dependency place and I take the test and it comes out I don't do drugs. I told them. I knew they wouldn't believe me. Sometimes I just look at 'em when they ask questions and then look away, don't say a thing. Or I pull my hair clear around to cover my face and hide from them.

They figure, hey, the kid has long hair, plays in a band, hates school, wears a leather coat, they think he's on drugs. I just laugh at 'em. Drugs are stupid. Have to be an idiot to spend money on drugs. I play the bass. I love playing the bass. The band. That's my drugs.

Looks, in Mike's case, were deceiving.

Jess, who looked like Mike, was another potential drug user. He was aggressive and would careen down the halls, slamming lockers shut while kids were reaching for their books. He'd slap his thighs to the beat of his drummer. About four times a minute, he'd flop his head forward and then quickly back, clearing his face of his hair. At those times we'd see a wide grin and his eyes blinking like 16th notes. This was often a prelude to hitting on some girl.

Jess liked girls a lot. He liked to impress them with his macho bravado or a tune from his Walkman™, which he'd share by holding one earphone close to the girl's head while sniffing her hair. This made him the envy of many other 15-year-old boys; but his eyes were frequently bloodshot, and he rarely controlled his talking. He was often tardy, but he never missed school. He was like a pinball in a School Building Game. He knew how to stay within the parameters, but made a noise wherever he touched.

Jess was the hardest kid to give up on. He could be funny and polite and bright; then he'd skip the last hour class or go smoke in the bathroom. Because of his hyperactivity, along with his bloodshot eyes, we wondered, is Jess on something?

Of course, there are many reasons why a student's behavior might be erratic. However, if we hope to modify behavior, it is reasonable to first wonder whether drugs are involved. If they are, our best efforts are usually doomed to failure. I wanted to be patient with Jess, to give him second chances as I deemed reasonable. But I was never willing to invest in him until it was determined that he was not abusing drugs. My history of working with untreated drug users has been one of heartbreak and failure.

Jess, we found out, was not a user. His eyes were reddened from shampoo residue, lack of sleep, and the tiny vessels that burst every 15 seconds as his eyeballs collided with their bony sockets. All this was exacerbated by the irritation smoke can cause sensitive tissue when one is confined to a bathroom stall.

They're not all on drugs, but some may be. It's chancy to accuse them based on their appearance. But appearance plays a part. It's not unfair to suggest a chemical evaluation when a youngster behaves erratically, fails in school, and dresses like a Mötley Crüe roadie. And it's imperative to find out before attempting any further behavioral interventions, for chemical abuse usually undermines any reasonable efforts to modify behavior.

Never Two Bad Days

Saturday night

Dear Tom,

This is a terrible time to write. I am momentarily depressed; poinsettias were on sale at Sears for $2.49, and we need six. I love poinsettias, and it was a bargain, but I was too tired to stop by and get any. Tomorrow, we get our tree. Poinsettias would have served as the warm-up band to the larger show. I've ruined Christmas.

As you see, Tom, I'm feeling sorry for myself. Reading your letter and thinking about the distress you are feeling with that class filled with special needs kids ought to shock me out of my own funk. So I thought I'd try writing through it and sending on to you my view of the situation and what I have done when facing a string of bad days.

First of all, you have an inordinate number of needy kids in one class, and though you think they must keep pace with your other classes, you have to be willing to retreat from that ideal. Success with them will have to be measured differently. It would be nice if they could read on their own, discuss material sensibly. But that is probably not possible just now. You will have to run this class in a way to ensure maximum output for the most kids; discussion and independent study will have to wait until each of them is part of a different class blend.

Since 1985, I have vowed never to have two bad days with a class in a row. I will do whatever is needed to ensure this doesn't happen. In the past, I have erred in lecturing a "bad" class about behavior. This fits their expectations and merely quiets them; it doesn't develop their resolve to improve. Now, I proceed instead with a highly structured, perhaps even tedious project that gives them immediate feedback and a sense of accomplishment. Such tasks are ordered in a pleasant, businesslike tone and followed by walking up and down aisles, looking over shoulders, commenting aloud, "I'm so impressed at how quickly you are all catching on here; let's only do the odd-numbered sentences in this exercise."

The letter to my teacher/friend continued with more suggestions.

What I have discovered after years of trial-and-error teaching is that if you want to regain control, or your sense that you have complete control, provide one full period of at-the-desk drills. The next day, read a story aloud and follow with a half-a-sheet-of-paper listening quiz.

The next day, assign a character description and, after showing a few examples, give them 25 minutes to think and write in class. When you graduate to independent (though clearly defined) writing assignments, everyone must write silently for 25 minutes. No talking, absolutely none. I keep the dreaded "language usage" packet to pass out if the talking starts; students who receive the packet will need to do the writing at home. Those who finish before the 25 minutes are up can proofread and then write in their journals; they can study their spelling words or use them in sentences or a creative story. But they are never done. Incidentally, if you are not using the Daily Point System with this group, start it on Monday.

This may never be a class you love. That's OK. What you need from them is attention to task. If they cannot handle oral or out-of-seat activities, keep them seated and silent. You may never get to read Romeo and Juliet with them or show them a video. You can keep trying the less-structured things you love best, of course, but always have alternative assignments that require only silent participation. Still, when you are matter-of-fact about assigning work and praise them for finishing it, they sometimes grow into your trust and favor. Their own sense of accomplishment sets each person apart from the other—the other who may have been allied with them in disrupting your class. You can get them back and on-track with your other classes; just don't require it of yourself. It is more important that they manage themselves in a way that meets your level of comfort.

I'm sorry to pontificate so, but already I'm feeling better. In closing, I raise the question again: Do you give a daily grade for time on-task?

Perhaps you will eventually have to find a sacrificial goat there—removing a ring leader—or stay with structure sentence-shaping or grammar tasks day in and day out. Or, maybe it's just count the days until the semester change and consider yourself blessed with the good classes you have. Some things we can't fix to our satisfaction.

Your Friend,
Benj

My colleague, Tom, needed to be reminded that we are not always miracle workers. Some classes won't keep up and won't like us, and we won't love them back. But the title premise remains: *Never have two bad days in a row.* Keep a file of favorite, no-fail assignments handy that can substitute for the next in-sequence assignment that had a miserable reception the previous day. For me, that may be reading a story aloud; kids always enjoy being read a story. It may be something with cut-and-paste potential, a personal poem, or essay of opinion. It may mean underlining all the nouns and circling all the adjectives on a packet of worksheets. Whatever you choose to do to avoid a second bad day should be something that affirms your sense of control. You must get them back, looking up to you, listening, knowing you give the grade, knowing you chart the course they are to follow.

Cutting Slack

I know when I'm using "power" techniques, because there is almost always a suppressed urgency; not infrequently, it is the urge to kill.

David, who was highly resistant to writing, balked at the rather simple, but open-ended task of expanding a general statement, like *The man was confident*, into a specific statement that would include gestures, expressions, and behavior that show confidence. David had mature, even eloquent verbal skills, and always wanted to respond orally to tasks that involved writing. He'd had so much applause on the home front for his precocious speech that he was unwilling to endure the physical stress of putting thoughts on paper. It was work. Talking had always been play.

We did this before.

These are different sentences. You won't be expanding the same ones as last time.

What the hell's the difference?

Now David, I know you meant heck.

No, I meant hell.

Of course he meant "hell." He meant *in-your-face-big-time-righteous-indignation-at-facing-busy-work hell.*

I suppressed an urge to be parental, to scold him for his comment (the one I provoked by glibly asking him to revise his feelings). But I had already erred once. I let this insolence pass over the *I-don't-have-to-take-that-tape* playing in my head. My throat burned with bile as he gave me a half grin, punctuating his little victory.

I thought, "What are the other kids going to think if I let this pass?"

Well, if this had been the first week of class, I'd use the "We'll talk later" approach. But, 25 weeks into the year, I know this little boy, and I realized his displeasure was not toward me, but the task, which he truly believed was tiresome and unnecessary. I said nothing, shrugged, smiled indulgently, and looked for others to follow his suit. No one did. David leaned his chin on his hand and gazed out the window at the snow melting in the March sun. The next day, he offered me complimentary tickets to see him perform—with brilliant irony—as the cowardly lion in a local production of *The Wizard of Oz*.

Freebies

Sarah had decided, in earnest, that she was going to pass English second semester. During the first semester, she'd been absent often enough that even her best intentions and a prolific journal could not get her a passing grade. Always, though, she had written and shared her journal with me. Twice every term she asked me questions—about friends, her family, her relationships with boys, the quality of her writing. I enjoyed writing back. She trusted me. Listened. Vowed to act on some of my suggestions. Thanked me.

Sweet, trusting Sarah. I knew she'd come through second semester on her promise of better attendance and with at least enough work to pass. I knew she would.

As the semester wore on, Sarah *mostly* kept her promise, but as she was still on the pass/fail border, I recommended she bolster her grade with some extra credit. Sarah responded with a fine effort.

She did additional readings on the Holocaust, and her written reactions were insightful and well-written. I was especially happy that she'd made a special effort on this unit. She showed me again, as she had in her journal, that she cared, that she had a good heart.

When I saw that Luke had also completed this optional assignment and that it matched Sarah's word-for-word, it was no contest in deciding who'd actually done the work. But was she coerced? I wanted to believe that he was going to force her to listen to an N'Sync tape if she didn't share her work.

Sarah, I said as I showed her the papers, each with a zero at the top.

Luke copied mine! she blurted.

Yes. I believe you. Does Luke often use people?

No!

I see.

I left her desk and walked back to deposit the fraudulent worksheets in the class folder.

Hmmm, I said.

Moments later, I approached Sarah again.

You know, Sarah, you have many good qualities to offer people that would not put yourself at risk.

I knew she understood exactly—sweet, lovable, cuddly, good-hearted Sarah. Tender, kind, searching, wanting-to-be-loved Sarah.

But Mr. Mahle, I offered it to him.

As advocates and parents, we can't help feeling we have failed when girls and boys relate this way. I wanted to despise Luke, but hey—he only took what was offered him. He'd have been an idiot to turn down a freebie, wouldn't he? Who taught us that?

Sarah could tell time, write well, do math, walk, draw stick people, analyze a poem, type on a computer. What is it that we needed to teach her that we didn't?

Writing Power Part 1: Staying Sane

To be able to save a life is a wonderful thing. Our teaching offers youngsters the chance to develop tools that improve lives, especially their own. To interest a youngster in soccer, playing the flute, woodworking, government, sculpture, growing plants, or architecture is, perhaps, to save a life. I teach writing for the nonwriter, the reluctant writer, the eager writer. My aim is to give each student a life-saving tool. I believe writing saves lives.

The gift of noticing happens through writing. Learning the names of things—putting them down to be reread and considered—gives the things of this world dignity and protection against the indifference of anonymity. A bluebird perches on rusted barbed wire by a weathered wooden fence post. With the gift of noticing, we can re-create life.

Writing also helps us to a bigger vision of what goes on inside of us. We learn to articulate what seemed too joyous or too horrible or too frustrating or too heartbreaking for words.

Writing scores high with kids in their final letters to me:

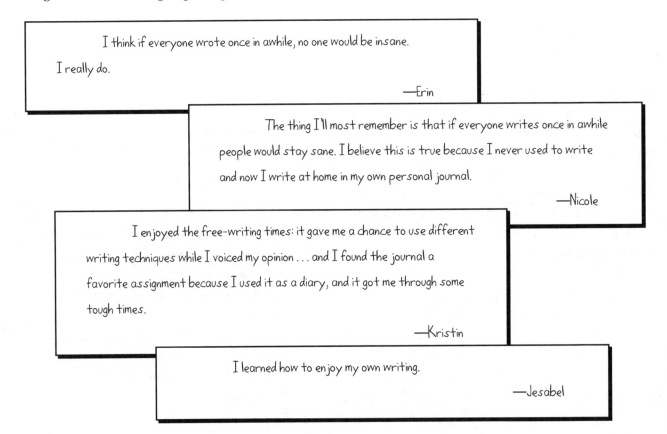

I think if everyone wrote once in awhile, no one would be insane. I really do.

—Erin

The thing I'll most remember is that if everyone writes once in awhile people would stay sane. I believe this is true because I never used to write and now I write at home in my own personal journal.

—Nicole

I enjoyed the free-writing times: it gave me a chance to use different writing techniques while I voiced my opinion . . . and I found the journal a favorite assignment because I used it as a diary, and it got me through some tough times.

—Kristin

I learned how to enjoy my own writing.

—Jesabel

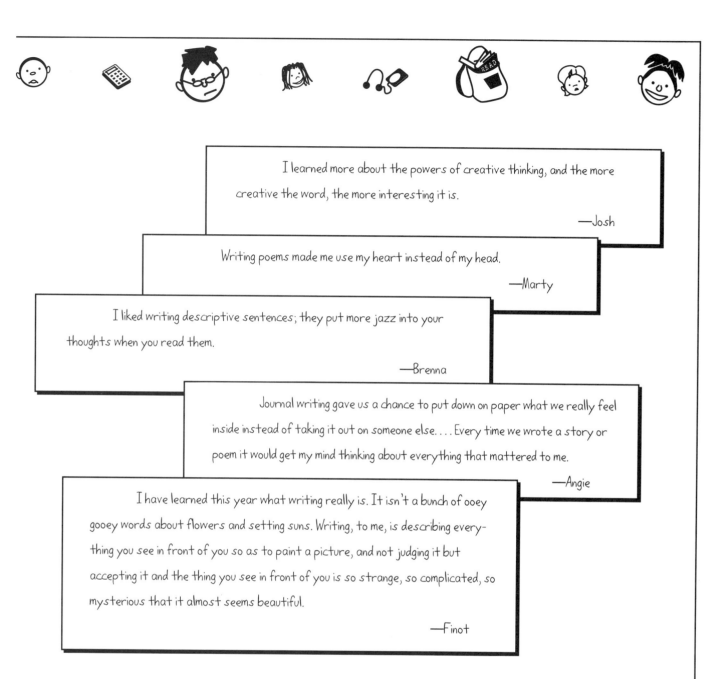

> I learned more about the powers of creative thinking, and the more creative the word, the more interesting it is.
>
> —Josh

> Writing poems made me use my heart instead of my head.
>
> —Marty

> I liked writing descriptive sentences; they put more jazz into your thoughts when you read them.
>
> —Brenna

> Journal writing gave us a chance to put down on paper what we really feel inside instead of taking it out on someone else.... Every time we wrote a story or poem it would get my mind thinking about everything that mattered to me.
>
> —Angie

> I have learned this year what writing really is. It isn't a bunch of ooey gooey words about flowers and setting suns. Writing, to me, is describing everything you see in front of you so as to paint a picture, and not judging it but accepting it and the thing you see in front of you is so strange, so complicated, so mysterious that it almost seems beautiful.
>
> —Finot

Writing teaches us to notice things in ways that make us care. *Caring* is the miracle we all want for kids, and for ourselves.

I won't say that all teachers must teach writing, though probably all teachers could encourage some writing when they have students account for the subject matter of the class. But I will say, without reservation, that all teachers will benefit from writing, if for no other purpose than to record specific details of their teaching lives. On a personal level, teachers can benefit for many of the reasons students have mentioned. Besides, it is one thing we can clearly do better than bears and seals. Writing gives the tongue-tied man a way to say *I love you*. We can take a problem, a pen, and some paper and write ourselves a solution. We can begin with a vague uneasiness or dread and discover through writing precisely what it is we fear.

Any of us can keep a journal. And now, computer journals are particularly convenient, given the comfort many of us feel with the keyboard. Journaling can help us become honest with ourselves. Even if we lie, we have the advantage of reviewing with ourselves what we've said through the physical presence of our thoughts. We can't do that with the spoken word or with the unexpressed musings that jumble up inside our minds next to grocery lists and which oil weight to use in the new lawn mower. Now and then, just sit at the keyboard and rest your fingers on the home row, lightly, like a bee pollinating a flower. Or brush your fingertips over the waxy surface of a new notebook, open it up, and see the lines awaiting your pen. Pick up a fast writing tool, like a fine-tip, rolling-ball pen, and begin. Ask your soul if it has something to say. And when you think it answers—as it will—quit being the teacher, the critic. Relax and trust the words that come easy.

One of the kids mentioned the value of free writing time. With free writing, you must observe one rule—Never stop moving the pen. If you are blocked about what to say, talk about the blockage—about the humbling, jarring reality of not being able to write on paper without pausing and thinking, *Geezwhothoughtthiscouldbesohard*? Eventually, you will get on to another thought, and if you allow yourself to run on, you will break through the barrier of self-criticism—which stops most of us from writing in the first place—and your heart will pour out through the wreckage of old posturings, and true diamonds, formed from years of your deepest, darkest feelings pressing inward, will be harvested right there on the page.

Free writing is usually done for a specific time period—begin with ten minutes at first—and is triggered by a starting sentence like *It was a time when I thought rain would last forever*, or *I turn with the leaves*, or *I remember. . . .* You can also begin with whatever is in front of you or on the floor of your closet. Describe the Looney Tunes® necktie curled

on top of your brown loafers and then say what you really wanted to tell Jamie, who arrived tardy for the third straight day smelling of cigarette smoke. Move on to the leak in the garage roof, your daughter's straight-A report card, the good news of your spouse's promotion. Start with noticing and move to what you are thinking, feeling, wishing, remembering. If you keep writing, you may inch toward the deepest truths, toward your soul. That would be like unraveling a great, furled roll of ribbon that we've been lucky enough to find the end of after picking around. That would be the page where you pause to breathe in, breathe out, let the ink dry, and say "Ah hah!"

Writing Power Part 2: Deep Down

I learned that in order to find out how you really feel, way deep down, you need to write and express yourself. Otherwise you'll never truly know. . . . I love the journal: I trusted you with my life and you respected me and showed me through both good and bad times. . . . I hope we can stay friends for a long time.

—Crissi

I particularly enjoyed the "Way down Deep" poems because they were hilarious to write and interesting to read.

—Hayley

I will most remember how you had us promise to give up a bad habit over the holidays. We had to do this for three weeks and then explain it to you in writing, how hard it was, how people reacted, etc. Even now I don't call my brother "butthead" anymore.

—Anonymous

Saturday night, 11:20 p.m.
January 6, 1990

Dear Tom,

I have spent most of today correcting the Christmas Memory project. It's the Capote story. The kids respond to the story and write their own memories; and then I've added things like earning extra credit for reading it with an older loved one, and doing "show of good spirit" projects too, such as eliminating derogatory expressions, or repairing a feud, or making sugar cookies for a neighbor, or shoveling his walk. . . . Reading these papers gives me a great pick-me-up, and will form the basis for a chapter of my sequel to Power Teaching (which has been started with this letter). . . .

Sincerely,
Benj

I realized, after writing the preceding letter to my teacher-friend Tom, that to sustain my spirit, I needed faith in kids, and especially in their basic humanity. I know some will fail me with broken promises, underachieve, steal a pencil daily, or heist the wrap-around sunglasses I keep on the file cabinet for sunny days of bus duty. I need to be reminded that these are a few kids, and even the toughest of them—once away from the competition of their peers and the need to pose "cool" and aloof—want to be human beings. They want to create beauty and joy and they want to give.

I realized through the Christmas Memory assignment that teachers—in fact, all adults—need to create situations that make it possible for kids to demonstrate their humanity without fear of having it exposed and ridiculed. We can all do this, teachers of every subject. We can't simply expect it to bloom in class discussions about things like racism or the environment.

In 1986, when the *Challenger* exploded, we had a rare silence on live television coverage as we all watched a wreath of smoke unfurl across the blue Florida sky. After a few minutes, this kid Rodney, watching, said, "Wasn't there a teacher on that?"

Yeah.
All right!

No play or film scene or moment from life to that point had ever made me want so badly to choke the life out of a human being. In that instant, I understood that part of man that has allowed him to scatter napalm on children or set off explosives next to a Federal building. I jerked toward him, briefly thinking I'd punch him full in the face. It seemed like his whole face was nothing but a huge eyebrow and a grinning mouth beneath. No eyes, no telling orbs. No personality or hint of life. Just this bushy mound of flesh-toned Silly Putty. I settled down, of course, but still wanted to punch his awful mouth into a splintered crater and set fire to his hair.

Over lunch that day, I worked through a batch of Christmas Memory assignments.

What follows on page 75 are examples of the kids' thoughts that saved Rodney, in my estimation, and me.

From Amanda:

This Christmas I thought who I could send a Christmas card to and my picture. I finally had thought of three different people who send me money or gifts through the mail. The next day I forgot to mail them out. When Xmas day came around I drove over to my grandma's and grandpa's and gave them a Christmas card with a picture of me from this year in it. Then I sat around awhile and just when I was leaving I pulled another envelope out and handed it to my grandma. She asked who it was for and I told her. She totally flipped out and asked me why I would decide to finally write or exchange a gift with my real dad after all these years and I just told her I couldn't be Grinch all of my life here on the planet earth.

From Emily:

I used to call my sister "stupid" all the time. I think it really put her down, and after awhile she began to believe me. I love my sister and I don't want to hurt her so when I get mad at her now I never call her "stupid" or imply that she's dumb. We haven't had a fight for two weeks. My mother is very happy, and so am I.

From Harry:

I have successfully eliminated a belittling comment towards my dad. I have gone through 10 days without saying something about his bald head. I am planning on never saying anything like that again because I figure if I lose my hair I will never hear the end of it.

From Vanny:

This Christmas holiday I create a card with bells and snowflakes all over and a small house under it and had wrote some special words on it and send it to my sister in Chicago. And 4 days later my sister called me and thanks me for the lovely card. She thought no one ever send her a card like that and I appreciated that she like the card that I send.

Vanny showed a special affection for Christmas. She read her Christmas Memory project with her father and three little brothers. This was her response:

When we talk about this story, my dad always think about his dad and his past and how happy they lived back then. (In Cambodia, before the war.) That make me wanted to be in the past to see how they are living. This story did remind me too of my little sister who died many years ago when I was a little kid. When I read about this story there are so many good things happening while we in our childhood experienced war, fighting, and bomb dropping every step we ran. Well now I'm glad to be here to share this Christmas past or Christmas memory.

It is easy not to acknowledge that everyone has a history. That may make teaching easier for some of us. But I need more than names and faces. I need to get inside kids' hearts and remember that who we see is not always who we are teaching.

Dan had trouble with teachers, especially women teachers. During the poetry unit he wrote this "Wish" poem:

> I wish
> I had a mother
> who liked me
> instead of always looking down on me
> with greater expectations.
> I wish
> I could live up to her standards
> of what a worthy person should be
> making her happy and proud.
> I wish
> I could take away her regrets
> of ever adopting a waste of hope
> like me.
> Also I wish
> that she would see me trying
> to please her, but she thinks
> I don't care what she thinks.
> I hope
> Someday she hears my plea
> and not think I'm thinking
> "Poor me."

Dan's poem waved a magic wand over me. After reading it, I saw him as someone different from the angry, leatherclad thug he appeared to be. He became instantly easier to like. I wrote "Wow!" on the poem and watched for some reaction when I handed it back. A slight "humphh," less than a sneeze, and then a slight upturn at the corners of his mouth. He'd accepted my encouragement. Dan became a better listener then, I think because he knew finally that he had been heard. It's too bad about appearances—Teachers must find ways to see inside.

At the change of semesters, I get a new collection of kids. Many of these students were well-satisfied with the teacher they had first semester and have no desire to switch. It is not uncommon to encounter a sort of sullenness during the first few days with new students. The sooner we can grow to like each other, the better.

At a workshop last spring, I discovered a short writing assignment to use with new classes. It is a simple nine-line form in which the first two and last two lines are the same. They begin:

Inside (or underneath) my _____
way down deep.

Tana, a ninth grader, was one of those sullen students. She responded to the writing assignment as follows:

Inside my heart
way down deep
it's quiet and lost
no one can see.
The outside is different
loud and selfish,
Who's the real me?
Inside my heart
Way down deep.

Amy, a quiet ninth-grade student, returned to me for second semester. I thought she was somewhat shallow first semester—she did decent, neat work, but didn't write with real feeling. Perhaps I hadn't given her the opportunity. When she was asked to complete the Way Down Deep assignment, she turned in this poem:

Inside my heart
Way down deep
White horses and waterfalls
A magical land where unicorns live
Truth and justice reign here
And there are eternal sunsets
I have hope in all the world
Inside my heart
Way down deep.

Simply stated, youngsters need permission to express attitudes, and they need acceptable parameters in which to do so.

Comparison and contrast exercises are another way to elicit opinions tempered with feeling. A ninth-grade student, Tana, chose to compare a sunrise and a sunset:

DIFFERENT

A sunrise is happier then a sunset because nighttime is scary and dark, and when the sun rises you can wake up, and forget all the horrible noises and shadows from the night. When the sun rises the day is just starting, and no one has made a mistake yet. Sunrises are happier because when the sun sets people have to leave each other sometimes, but when the sun rises people can get back together to start their day with each other. Doctors say breakfast is the most important meal of the day because it happens right after the sun rises. The most time I spend with my dad is in the morning when the sun is rising. That's when we go fishing. Everyone knows sunrises are happier than sunsets because kids draw the bright sunrise with a smiley face. My cousin died when the sun was setting, and that's why sunrises are happier then sunsets, because better things happen after a sunrise.

Everyone has a history. Carefully chosen assignments can get at that history and help define the attitudes that each individual's past has helped shape. We will be part of each child's past. Hopefully we will have given them the chance to remind us that they are human beings, for it makes teaching them such a much more hopeful and happy task.

Your Castle

My classroom is one of my favorite places. It is large enough to host a tennis match. One enormous bulletin board runs nearly 30 feet along the south wall. On it is posted a collection of student work and memorabilia cast against a background of construction paper in multiple colors, including goldfinch yellow, royal blue, orange, black, white, radish red, purple, golf course green, and flamingo pink.

"Hermann" and "Lockhorns" cartoons still amuse me and student readers even as the edges have yellowed. Students have added favorites from "Garfield" and "The Far Side." I laugh every time I notice the drawing of two spiders, one with a web of kaleidoscope symmetry spread out behind him and wearing a mask; the other, his web curled beneath him like a snarl of fishing line, is fielding a question from the masked one:

Gee, I guess I really scared you, eh Bob?

My room is a web. I want it to be a web. I want it to draw kids in and hold them. It's done with humor and color and theme.

My favorite part of the room is the collection of student work—type-written poems glued on a shape cut from several colors of paper that symbolize the various tones of the writer's personality. Red for anger or passion; yellow for the softer, mellower moments; black for the down days; gold for the days of triumph and joy.

Other work may include riddles or poems documenting the "Little Joys of Life." Short "note card reviews" of movies or books that kids have seen or read are displayed on index cards. Students pause frequently to admire their own stuff or that of friends.

I often post newspaper articles about subject matter of interest to teens—a school board proposing to abolish homework; a proposal to *require* homework; a principal not being compensated for taking an assailant's bullet while protecting a class of students; teen accidents involving drunk driving; student-of-the-month clippings; academic and athletic honors involving kids we all know.

A faded valentine from three girls, class of 1979. A teacher-of-the-week award. A watercolor by a student from 1981 depicting a road sign and the order "Keep Right" is posted to the left of the room's only exit. Another student drawing that shows an ancient Salem dunking stool and the definition of *catch-22*—a situation in which one fails no matter which action is taken.

But the best feature of the room is the kids. Every day they arrive with their interests, problems, confusion, and guilt—and, in a back pocket, the proof of their friendships folded four times in a note. They come in wearing signs implicit in the way they dress: *Rock 'n Roll Addict, Sports Nut, Fashion King or Queen, Fragile. Handle With Care.* (They could all wear that last one at some point.) And then I'm onstage, in charge, and they give me a moment to recognize them and arrest their attention. Any of these kids in my room could spend a full period just mulling over the problems and decisions in their lives, but when they first arrive, I have a chance to push away those concerns and say, "Good morning." Then it's up to me to see that we make it a good morning. The room is important to that end.

I will pick on math teachers now. Why are your rooms so much like the interior of a breadbox? Do you think color and form will distract these kids from the business of fractions? Surely you can devise projects that will enable your students to see their work displayed. Admittedly, it's easy enough in English—but as for you English teachers out there who only display definitions for the parts of speech, shame! Yes, I see English classrooms dull as tombs. If your room does not speak of who you are and what you do, you've missed a great way to enhance your personal power.

People are indifferent toward anonymity, which is why we have to instruct them to not litter in public places. Did you know that stretches of highway that have been "adopted" engage half as much litter as those bearing no specific designation? Of course, you can demand that your room be kept neat and clean—I hope you do—but wallpapering your room with the work of your students enlists them in caring about what the place looks like and what goes on there. You do want students to care, don't you?

Last year, I moved from my great room at Kellogg Junior High School. Kellogg had become a middle school, grades 6–8. I packed up my ninth-grade materials and headed for a building that had once been a furniture store. It would house ninth graders only—for math, English, and American history. For the first time in 23 years, I was without windows. How would I survive without the hillside of my Kellogg environs, the spring lilacs, the golds and oranges and sumac reds of fall? I would

miss seeing the student trails cut into the hill for kids who lived just above and the occasional skulking truant who we'd spot and holler at out the window: "You're busted!"

I was sick to my stomach through the first two days. I told the kids:

I'm feeling very homesick for my old Kellogg school. I especially miss the windows. I miss daylight and the cafeteria workers who chatted and washed pans on the loading dock below, the dipsty dumptster™ truck emptying the garbage, banging the huge metal box until the last of those sticky ketchup packets fluttered down from the floor of the dumpster and safely into the truck's bed.

You're going to have to help me. You're going to have to make some windows in here, some shapes and color that will make me forget my old place.

And they did. The second day we wrote the two-tone "personality poems," and students cut and pasted personality into my room. I haven't missed the open windows of Kellogg since. This room became mine, theirs, and never a day passes that one student or another doesn't pause and point, "Hey here's mine! See mine?" You empower others when you give them ownership, especially when they have a chance to own the art, beauty, symbols of the joy and confusion, heartaches, mayhem, and triumphs that adolescents live and breathe on any given day.

Your room is where you will spend most of your daily life. Make it mean something to you; it will then mean something to kids! When you personalize things important to you, you have the tremendous power of caring spread out there to protect those things against litter, casual assault, or indifference. Your caring infuses the population of children, which then sees you and your room as one humanized unit to be valued and respected. Include the art and science work of those kids in the decor of your room, and they will know you've noticed. They will be flattered and want more of it. Students are thrilled when an adult allows them inside such a room.

Your room can speak to the learning that goes on there. Your room can be a testimonial to the students and teachers who are framed by those four walls. Your room can illuminate and inspire— the way real windows and a view will.

Insurance

Here's a subject you are likely to never hear about in graduate school. It's something you learn along the way, after talking to fellow teachers. It's a just-in-case safety net that gives me the confidence to do my job better.

For $25 a month, a rider on my insurance policy gives me a million dollars of coverage against any professional liability. This peace of mind allows me to mostly ignore the occasional irrational threat, "Touch me and I'll sue!"

Students who are out of control may need to be physically restrained. That fact wouldn't change regardless of insurance I may have purchased or the silliness of some courts in this land. Knowing I'm insured, though, dispels second thoughts about what is reasonable and right and frees me to do what my presence in any situation requires.

Contact your local teacher's union for more information or talk to your colleagues in the teacher's lounge to find out what kinds of coverage are available in your area.

The Squeaky Wheel

Cory and Rob were similar students. Both were tall and gawky and usually entered the room with smiles when I met them at the door with a nod and a greeting, "Gentlemen." Mostly, they were. They were never crude or threatening the way posturing adolescents can sometimes be. Neither of them was bold enough to interact much with the girls in the room, and both were shy about offering answers in class. I liked them. They worked hard every day.

And every day they tried to drive me crazy.

Does this look OK, Mr. Mahle? Does the paper need a title? Where do I put my name? Should I cut the ragged edges off the first draft, too? Does this have to be in ink? Will we get these back tomorrow? Look at how neatly I wrote this; aren't you impressed? Isn't that neat? I'll bet it's the neatest paper you've got yet, isn't it? Is it OK to write on the back? How is this for a title? Didn't you say the paper had to have an interesting title? Well, how do I know if it's interesting?

Everyday they buzzed around me with questions I'd already answered at least 12 times.

I never investigated why these boys needed my attention and approval 17 times a day. We seldom have time to explore nuisance behaviors in that way. We all have had students who need constant reassurance. However, answering mundane questions repeatedly is not the way to give approval and reassurance. Nor is it your job.

The old adage *The only dumb question is the one not asked* had stuck with these boys from early on. I would like to boil in oil the sage who created that old saw. There *are* such things as dumb questions. Questions for which we've already given the answer four billion times are dumb. And how smart am I for answering time after time? Not too. Moreover, the dependency this creates with the questioner slows his or her maturity.

I finally figured out what to do with kids like Cory and Rob. First, I try to acknowledge the person before the questions begin: "Nice shoes, Cory. You go fishing this weekend? How about those Timberwolves! Hey, you want to pass back some papers?" This often helps satisfy the need for attention. Still, I can depend on a myriad inquiries from the overly conscientious boys as soon as an assignment is given.

Cory, I explained about the ragged edges and the title. I've done that every time I assign a composition.

I know. I forgot.

I'm sorry. I have to encourage you to remember. So, here's the deal—You can ask me two questions a day.

What?

That's one; you have one left. You may want to save it for later.

But . . . but . . . you're saying we shouldn't feel free to ask questions?

Would that be your second question then?

Ah, no! No! It's just that, well, teachers are supposed to answer questions.

Students are supposed to listen to directions.
That's not fair.
No, it's a circus!
Ha. Ha.

And Cory returns to his seat, looks up and stares at the dog prints in the tile ceiling above him where, in time, the answers appear, and I see him writing again.

Everyone in the room is aware of the rightness of this policy; they see how it allows openings for other students to ask *their* questions. The child's parents know it's fair, as do former teachers, friends, and everyone else who has suffered for this child's rambling diet of *wheres*, *what abouts*, *hows*, and *whens*.

Putting an end to pestering questions is an act of compassion. First, it forces the child to actually think before speaking. This is a wonderful habit for persons of any age to develop. Second, removing the mundane and obvious from the atmosphere creates a slightly more thoughtful and intellectual setting, and invites kids in the class to offer new ideas. But most importantly, it creates distance between you and the student, giving you a chance to like him or her so much more.

Sometimes a student will ask inane questions merely to get the attention of the group or to mimic you or to play dumb. The "two question limit" works for that situation as well.

Mr. Mahle, you said we could turn our essay in on time and earn points for it and get credit as well, but that late assignments only get credit, no points.
That's correct, Rob.
So, do you think I should turn it in on time?
Guess what, Rob.
What?

I'm putting you on a two question limit today, and you just used one. Do you really want to spend the other one on the question about your essay?
That's not fair!
Are you asking me if limiting you to two questions is fair?

Pause. *No.*

When you've been reasonable about helping kids, you needn't concern yourself with the fairness issue. As stated before, kids want justice in life, not fairness (otherwise they'd have to share their video games, stereo systems, and starter jackets with the third-world poor). The "two question" strategy urges immature students to think of *real* questions and puts the smart alecks out of the business of playing dumb.

Seating

A student named Jessica took her assigned seat in the middle of the third row. From the beginning, it was a mistake. She was too cute and too fond of the attention she received from the nearby boys. Jessica never heard a thing I said. She always thought it was better to engage one of the charged young fellows around her after I'd delivered instructions: "What did he say? What page?"

On the third day, I moved her to the front of the room, five feet from where I usually delivered instructions. It didn't help. She was still the center of attention. I moved her to a corner seat in the back row, the furthest point from my voice. From there, she had no one to ask. She became totally dependent upon her own listening. Moreover, she didn't want to ask me to repeat things; that would make her look dumb. She simply began to listen from there, rows away from any enabling by me or by others.

There's no law that says a student can't be moved until you find just the right place. It behooves you, the child, and the rest of the students to resolve trouble spots caused by unworkable seating arrangements. While your intentions when you mapped out the seating chart may have been sound, if the seating doesn't work, be willing to make adjustments. Eventually, you'll stumble upon a seat where the Jessicas of your classroom will have fewer distractions and be able to focus on learning.

Candy Man

Kids sometimes come to class in awful shape. We all know this. Monday morning, Trina looked like she'd slept the previous night in a wagon rut.

You look kinda bummed out today, Trina.
Uhmmmm.
Anything I can do?
Uhmmmm.

I pulled a toffee from my desk drawer—I keep them there for myself—and I walked back to Trina's desk and laid it next to her hand.

This is from my "bummed out" file.

Not everyone likes candy, but even the few who don't will like a melt-in-your-mouth butter candy. Trina slipped the wrapper off slid the candy into her mouth.

I don't allow candy in class, and I never give candy away to kids except in life-or-death situations. Trina had something frozen in her stomach—an anvil, maybe, or a collection of last straws from the boys in P.E. who called her "dogface," and from her dad who missed his visitation for the fourth straight Sunday. Trina was so low that her raven hair lay like a tire skid across her forehead. You've seen her. You want to help, but what she most needs extends beyond the classroom boundaries. She needs a stable home and a healthy sense of herself.

There are things beyond a teacher's control, issues that can't be fixed in a classroom period. Instead, I gave Trina a piece of candy. It was a simple act of caring. It wasn't so much to do.

Notes

I love notes. Teachers brag about how they discourage note-writing by confiscating notes and pinning them on the bulletin board. That's fine. When I observe a note-writer, I consider what else the person has to do in class. What is so much less pressing than this note? I consider how I use writing—to get through problems, to sort out issues in my life, to vent. Why should I assume Danielle is doing anything less in her note? I can tell when it's frivolous. She looks up to see if I'm watching. She is not stern-faced, intent. But when the pen presses hard onto the paper and the writing is fast, something strong is working itself out of that little girl. I let it go and stop for a note of my own.

Dear Danielle,

I can see this writing is pretty important to you. Can you promise me you'll finish your assignment at home tonight? Then I don't have to feel bad about not interrupting you and having you work on it now. Circle one response and please return this to me.

Yes, I promise.   No, I make no promises.

Letters given to students mid-class can be effective in a variety of circumstances. Such as the following one I wrote to a chatty boy:

Dear Tom,

I see you are having a real tough time not talking with Bob during the showing of <u>The Elephant Man.</u> Would it be better if I had you come in after school to watch it, when Bob will be at basketball practice? Or can you separate from Bob and concentrate on the film?

Please move from Bob now to a different seat if this makes sense to you.

Dear Andrea,

I don't think you are cheating on this test, but you have a habit of looking to your left a lot, toward Joy's paper. Could you please look straight ahead when you're thinking? Thanks.

Dear Seth,

Jennifer seems pretty uncomfortable with some of the things you are whispering to her. Are you being appropriate? Do we need to discuss your comments with her parents or yours? Maybe you'd like to ignore Jennifer for the next week or two.

Dear Kami,

I think your socks are cool.

I write notes to kids whenever they need input from me that I don't want to share orally with the rest of the class. It lets the kids know you're paying attention. It's an easy thing to do.

You Are What You Do

Tom:

That Chris, he is a no-good kid. He lies and steals. Plain and simple, he's no good.

I'm thinking:

Chris writes poetry. It's pretty deep, some of it. Pretty good, too.

Tom:

Same with that Bill kid. He stole a van last summer, wrapped it around a tree; and I guess he's a big shot in that white supremacist group, the punks called the All-American Boys.

I'm thinking:

I never would have guessed; Bill asks about assignments and never otherwise opens his mouth. He's had a B all year.

Chris is a poet who steals or a thief who writes poetry. Bill is an honor student with a felony conviction or a racist felon with good grades. Tom is partly right—for after all, we are what we do. Why separate the person from the act? It's easier to accept people as imperfect than to pretend that the person who steals is somehow better than that. That's the stupidest thing I've ever been told teachers ought to do.

Eva Braun could love Hitler for his kindness to dogs and the sketches he drew of the Austrian Alps. But don't tell me that means he had a good heart. Some troubled kids have good hearts, and you'd never suspect. But in the long run, that won't be enough. It's like the ancient grandparent on his deathbed, stoic to the end, his children and grandchildren surrounding him, counting his breaths. "I know he loved us," Martha whimpers. "He just never could show it."

He never said it either. How then did she know? He treated the kids like employees, never once thanked any of them or his wife for a kindness. Never complimented a meal or a good catch in the outfield. Never attended a game or a concert. "He was a good provider," Audrey remarks. "He always paid his bills."

Sorry ladies; the old boy didn't love anyone, 'pears to me.

We are what we do; we are what we appear to be. People can't guess at our good hearts. We have to *show* that we have them. Good hearts—not perfect. Tom's heart is good; he coaches for free, runs a Boy Scout troop. I have a good heart. So probably do you. Don't doubt it just because you judge students by the wrong they do. We can like them better when they change. The only way people can change is to change what they do. We need to encourage that. Another person's acts may change how we view him or her. I believe that is how it ought to be.

You can like or not like a particular person—and I tell kids these same things—and you can feel any way you want about a group. No one can tell you how to feel. You can be a bigot and a racist and you can even hate dogs until something changes your mind. You would be wise, however, to think long and hard before acting on any of those feelings and before letting your preferences show.

Students in my classroom must respect each other, or pretend to. I would love to have genuinely unbiased persons around me at all times, and would love to be one myself. Until that happens, however, we must settle for "pretend." If that makes us phonies, so be it. I think we are, instead, actors. We pretend the poem is good, the drawing, the new hairdo, the school picture. We master the ambiguous comment: "How interesting! Oh, wow! Bet you're proud of that, eh?" We are not liars then, but actors—some with good hearts.

Put-Downs

Sometime before this year is out, I hope to find out from one of you why kids pick on each other so much and then tell me in their writing that being put down is the most hurtful thing about their school day.

We'd been doing activities to help us see the subtle as well as the obvious forms of discrimination. Gabe raised his hand. I knew he'd been on both the giving and receiving ends of discrimination. I looked his way and saw the serious tone of his face slide into a smile: "I know," he said confidently. "It's because then in school there would be no comedy."

Gabe is right—an insult is usually funnier than a compliment. We seem to laugh almost naturally at misfortune that creates minor discomfort. Few of us think decapitations or torn spleens are riotous. But yes, we grin at awkwardness, stumbling, faces changing color. The best thing we can do is insist that kids refrain from picking on other kids for conditions over which they have no control. If you defend the most unfortunate child in this way, others will adopt your view. The climate will change. Comedy will find other forms. "No put-downs" is a reasonable expectation.

Thinkin', Blinkin', and Nod

Kids come to your class tired for a variety of reasons. If a student nods off on consecutive days, ask why, and document the response. On the third day, make contact with the office so they can check for problems at home.

Spotting the occasional napper needn't make you panic about your delivery, or even the material itself. Kids can get drowsy in most school settings. A simple corrective comment will suffice. Ask Fred if he'd like to get a drink of water. If he does and continues to drift even then, ask him to stand at the back of the room until he wakes up. Finally, if he really can't keep from nodding off, he must be sent to the nurse. All these measures can be done without scolding or raising your voice. Being tired is not insubordination or insolence, and you must avoid taking it personally.

Movie and video presentations tempt even your best students to grab a little shut-eye. When the lights go off, the shutters will come down for more than a few unless there is a car crash or threat of violence within the first 30 seconds. When heads slip sidewise to the desks, move with stealth and purpose and get the students standing. That's the best way to engage them.

Jake, please stand until you are sure you can stay awake.

Once in awhile, a student will complain that the video is just too boring. Before he or she can express that feeling, it might be best to say this:

Sandy, I know you are feeling sleepy, but if you drift off during this tape, you will give the other kids the impression that you are not interested in serious topics. Do you really want them to think that about you?

No. I'm sorry.

Sandy will then do her best to stay awake. But remember, most teenagers come to school with some sleep debt. After-school jobs, sporting and musical events, socializing, and homework combine to short kids on the sleep they need. You needn't let them catch up in your class, but don't pass judgment on them. Of course, if your classroom sounds like it's filled with muffled power saws five minutes into your lesson plan, you maybe ought to look to improve your presentation.

That's Stupid!

For several years I've shown a film called *The Wave*, wherein a high school teacher manipulates his history class into following his dictates in much the same way Hitler duped the German people. It is a ridiculous premise to many kids, who think themselves far too savvy to either join something or get excited about it. During a recent showing of *The Wave*, my class was engaged in a seemingly negative way. They mocked and ridiculed the film's characters and their salutes and enthusiasm for their group (the Wave). I had to stop the film.

Pretty ridiculous, huh?

No kidding, man. Who dreamed this up?

It's a true story.

Yeah, right.

And you are all bright enough to see the point, right? I can see that by your reactions to the behavior of the students. They are really acting stupidly. We find it pretty amusing.

I can't believe high school kids could go along with that stuff, I mean, saluting? Getting in fights over the Wave?

Pretty dumb.

So, why are we watching this?

The students in this story had just spent several weeks studying Nazi Germany. Afterwards they were troubled by the claim made by many Germans that they knew nothing of what was happening to others around them. The students asked, "How can this be?" And yet within days, their teacher duped them in almost the same way.

Stupid.

Exactly. They didn't see the possibility for something like this to happen in their own lives. They were stupid for joining the Wave, sure. No one is trying to show you otherwise. But can you tell me how this happened to them?

They were stupid.

How many of you have worn the uniform of a group, recited allegiances or oaths, pledged to uphold the goals of the group, or put friends and family matters aside in order to attend a meeting or a practice? How many of you have heard things like, "Sure, a few people will be put out (or hurt) a little; but it's for the good of the whole?" *Can you see similarities between your group, gang, or team and the Wave?*

Not really.

Most of you can't, because you were too occupied with thinking of clever ways to ridicule those other kids. When you ridicule someone, it clouds your view of the reasons why they are behaving as they do. When you ignore the causes of behavior, you risk behaving that way yourselves, and that makes you stupid. We must not let our urge to ridicule distract us from thinking about the causes of "stupid" behavior.

In brief, counter the comment "This is stupid" with "Can you tell me exactly why it's stupid?" or "What do you mean by 'stupid?'" Take a close look at the rest of the film so you can share your opinions when we are through. When students answer a request for specific reasons with the generic "It's stupid," they are substituting emotion for thinking. By agreeing with them, and then asking for more explanation, you placate the "emotional" students in the group, while empowering the "thinkers" to take over. "That's stupid" is an expression of frustration or confusion; it is not a personal attack on you.

Any School You Want

You can have any kind of school you want. I am absolutely convinced of this. You, your colleagues, your administrators, and your students and their parents can create and maintain any kind of school that all of you decide you want.

Most of what I have said in this book applies to managing your teaching and supervisory assignments. But there is a broader view to consider, and I feel every teacher has a professional obligation to look long at the climate of the building where he or she resides. This may be stating the obvious; however, I was a "new" teacher for several years, and many things were not "obvious."

What has since become obvious is that schools are run from the top down, and the attitude and philosophy of the top person affects how employees and clients will feel. The platitudes of these higher-ups, when backed by decisive (and sometimes fierce) action, will become the attitudes of that school.

Take hats. More specifically—as stated elsewhere—take them off.

My new principal, J. W., hated hats. Many of us didn't care to have kids wearing hats either. But compared to the street language and behavior that pervaded the halls of our junior high at that time, hats seemed a minor issue. I thought J. W. was pretty naive to want to tackle hats then. We were a school of about 1,000 students. The staff controlled the climate for learning in their individual classrooms, but the halls were horrible—filthy with papers and food wrappers, with scribbling on lock-

ers and the dandruff of broken ceiling tiles that were punched to death several times a week. Teachers had largely retreated to their rooms. The language was an even greater embarrassment. Kids weren't shy about the f-word and showed no remorse when confronted about it. In 1989, many staff had given up the halls.

It wasn't J. W.'s fault or the fault of the assistant principal. Rather, the superintendent and the school board had let us down. The new "supe" had ridden into town on a very high horse, deciding in advance that what our school system needed was Outcome-Based Education (OBE) and government-by-committee. The building principals bore the brunt of this philosophy, and some were assigned as many as seven committees. That they should spend time in their respective school buildings became a secondary consideration. Moreover, our district had long been arrogant and dishonest by suggesting that discipline problems really didn't exist in our schools, that the negative behaviors were mischievous at worst.

Newsletters home never mentioned behavioral concerns. Of course it's good to emphasize the positive, the high percentage of honor-role names and huge array of extra-curricular activities offered by each school. But parents ought to get all the news through a newsletter. The climate of a school should be evident in these communications home.

In truth, we'd had vandalism and food fights and assaults that the community in general new nothing about. So personally, I laughed cynically when J. W. mentioned hats at a faculty meeting. I asked him, "Would the office suspend kids who were insolent and insubordinate in not complying with our requests?"

As I remember, there was no agreement then on consequences. Instead, J. W. mentioned that the disciplinary tool currently in force could be used.

The staff sighed. Same-old, same-old. Our vice principal, a very bright woman, and the hardest working administrator I've ever known, was saddled with a discipline policy that a very conscientious committee had worked hard at developing a year or so before she'd arrived. Unfortunately, this policy, designed to get tough with kids, had so many contingencies as to be unworkable. Essentially, various offenses were given a point value, and at some point, a cumulative score earned the perpetrator a particular consequence. The design of the policy was insidious in its delegation of responsibility to the administration, and some teachers abused the spirit of the policy by referring kids to the office for things such as not bringing a pencil to class. This plan grouped incompetent kids with incorrigibles in a gross melting pot of bad-tasting language and dress, which office secretaries then had to control. Every day, a conglomeration of children—some naughty, some sleepy or forgetful, and some genuinely criminal—oozed and fidgeted outside the vice principal's office.

The job was overwhelming. It shouldn't have been. But we had advertised ourselves as the school district with the finest students, staff, and administrators in the Midwest. We were first on the cutting edge of nationally known educational specialist Madeline Hunter, and then OBE. And we hadn't expelled a kid in ten years.

When the new "supe" arrived, he began a huge project with great merit that involved dozens of teachers and community members. The committee was called the Strategic Long-Range Planning Committee (SLRP). Through many months and hours of meetings, this group assessed the needs of students in the district in terms of curriculum, technology, and building facilities. SLRP wrote a document of several hundred pages with detailed academic objectives and curricular expectations for the students of our district, and projections of what kids would need in order to learn over the next ten or more years. While this was surely a worthy study in many respects, nowhere in the document was there any mention of behavioral expectations or objectives. With the SLRP document in print, the school board and the new superintendent had officially taken the road most traveled by previous boards and administrators, and declared that our district was a unique system in a unique community where none of the kids were really all that bad. No mention of behavioral objectives for students in a long-range plan that would impact 12,000 kids a year!

This community was continuing to walk blind and deaf around its schools. Communication from schools continued to be fraudulently positive. I know for a fact that in our building were at least 20 juveniles who were in the criminal justice system for having committed felony offenses. These kids did things every day in and around our school that would get an adult on the street arrested.

The street was alive in our building. One student smoking a cigarette walked past a colleague on the fourth floor. He approached her, blew smoke in her face, and said, "Fake cigarette." She followed the boy who, still smoking, stopped on the third floor and crushed the cigarette out in the carpet.

A female colleague was followed by a group of five boys who chanted *whore, whore, whore* until she reached her room.

The vice principal was screamed at and called a "f___ing bit____" in front of the entire lunch room.

A bomb threat was called in from our lobby phone, one of half a dozen that year.

Students regularly were sexually and physically harassed. Conduct was generally vile, and the building was regarded by students with indifference, animosity, or disgust. In one seventh-grade food fight, seven plastic trays were broken.

A young man came to my third-hour class drunk.

A smoke bomb was set off in a classroom.

Substitute teachers refused to return to our building. Teachers living in our area sent their kids to other junior high schools.

Spitting was common. A student spitting in another student's face was not unheard of.

Staff concerns were met with interest by our principals, but our common chant—*Get these kids out of here*—did not reflect a disciplinary philosophy that our school district embraced. There was little precedent or encouragement for suspending "bad" kids; our board was ignorant, and our administrators downtown were arrogant in downplaying negative behavior. The superintendent pretended to empathize with our plight, then told us we were self-governing and to work our problems out at the building level. Ultimately, this was his only gift to us.

I've said you can have any school you want. You can.

The superintendent's injunction angered us at first; then we said, "Well I guess it's up to us to row our own boat." We formed a Climate Committee.

The first step in changing our school was to ask J. W., the principal, how serious he was about the hat thing. "Hats drive me nuts. Isn't anyone else bothered by these?" This told us that he did not favor having our school be an extension of the street. The committee now believed change was possible in our building and would be supported by our two principals. After our meeting with the superintendent, J. W. was able to clear time from district committees and spend more time with us. Next, we needed to discover what kind of school our staff wanted to have.

Our first committee survey found that the staff's overwhelming concern was insubordination. By a vote of 57-to-1, we found that staff thought a student who is warned in a reasonable way, but who persists in defying staff, is insubordinate and should be suspended. Blame it on poor parenting, low self-esteem, too little sleep, sugary breakfast cereal—in any case, such students should experience "time out" away from the building. This supported our Climate Committee's belief that nothing more quickly demoralizes school personnel than the sense that children can mock them with impunity. Morale among our staff was lower than a snake's belly in a wagon rut. Nothing would change that short of *seeing* change.

Now that we had documented the feelings of our staff, we on the committee knew the next step was to get them out in the halls again, *regardless* of what our principals might do to support us, and regardless of whether or not certain kids would be removed from the building for insubordination.

The committee issued the letter on pages 98–100 to fellow staff members. The response was encouraging.

The majority of the staff supported our requests, but lurking in the minds of each veteran

TO: All Staff
FROM: Climate Committee

Dear Staff:

Thank you for returning the survey of last week. Your concerns and comments were most enlightening and have given the committee impetus for acting on your priorities. It is clear that each of you has one or more issues that are personally sensitive. For the remainder of this school year, we would like to focus on one: out-of-classroom behavior.

You have indicated an overwhelming concern with the issues of swearing, loud and abusive language, inappropriate touch, loitering/tardiness, and student challenges to reasonable direction and correction. The tone and volume of your responses communicate clearly that changes in kids' behaviors here are essential if each of us is to enjoy a career (or even a day) in this building. Something else is clear: Most of us have at some time felt powerless in confronting inappropriate behavior in the halls. We have departed from these situations feeling steamed and humiliated, and have then had to carry these feelings into our classrooms. We want abrupt and severe consequences for those kids who've made us feel this way, and, when perceiving that this has not happened, we are discouraged from intervening in future incidents. After all, who needs more humiliation?

Yet your survey responses indicate that we need to do more teaching in the halls than anywhere else. We need to make the building more livable—a gentler, kinder place—and that will not happen by retreating from intervention or by laboring under the delusion that we are specialists and teach only English, or math, or French, or science, or physical education, or music, or sewing, or art, or health, or German, or Spanish, or band, or history, or special ed., or . . . you get the idea. We hope support staff can also become more comfortable in offering kids correction and direction. However, teachers must be the examples for this. To these ends, we would like commitments from all teachers these last few weeks to doing the following:

-1-

1. Usher your students in and out of your classrooms, and remain in the halls as classes pass.

2. Ask kids who are found in the halls after the tardy bells ring where they are supposed to be.

3. Supervise out-of-classroom areas in pairs: kids are less likely to challenge "teams" of us.

4. Follow-up on insubordinate behavior before referring it to the office.
For instance, if a student is defiant and unreasonable when confronted, seek him/her out during your free period. Confront the person one-to-one, such as the following example:

> "Why did you walk away from me?"
> "I thought you were done talking to me."
> "You weren't just trying to show off for your buddies?"
> "No. I really thought you were done with me."
> "Then, if I explained to you a signal I give kids when I'm done talking with them, and you learned that signal, then I could expect you'd not have the problem of walking away from me if we should talk again sometime?"
> "Huh?"
> "I'm asking if you could remember a simple signal I give kids that lets them know when I'm done talking with them."
> "Yeah. Sure."
> "So the next time we talk you'd know when we're finished."
> "Yeah. Sure."
> "That's good. I know you'll not have the problem of walking away from me then, because the signal is simple."
> "Yeah?"
> "Yeah. When I'm done talking with you I'll just say, 'See ya later.' Got that?"
> "Yeah."
> "Good. See ya later."

-2-

Of course, it is hard to do this while grinding one's teeth or while foaming at the mouth. But if you can avoid trying to handle this kind of insubordination with the whip and truncheon it probably deserves, you will communicate a more real sense of your control to the student. Moreover, if we can relieve the office of dealing with insubordination of this degree, they can commit more time and energy to confronting kids who defy us with threats, swearing, and so on.

Please make a commitment to teamwork, to team-teaching here. Let's see if in these last weeks we can impact student behavior with our presence and our vigilance in the halls. We needn't be dramatic if we are simply all there. Please fill out and detach the slip below, and return it to the wire basket in the office.

Respectfully,
The Climate Committee

- -

The Climate Committee suggestions seem reasonable, and I will attempt to comply. (Name optional) _____.

I cannot/will not comply with all/part of these suggestions, for the following reasons:

_____

_____

-3-

of the previous two years was this question: *Will doing these things make a difference, or will it be the "same old" with kids who we refer for suspendible offenses returning moments later, haughty and smirking, heading to their next classes with slapped wrists?* We knew staff involvement could help the building in the short term, but that for long-term interventions to continue, our teachers would have to know that J. W. and our assistant principal were going to deal out some suspensions.

About this time, a "racial" incident put our school in the news. In the aftermath, 12 students were suspended. The community began asking questions about our school. The "supe" decided J. W. should spend even more time onboard with us. Soon he was in the building so much that the wearing of hats by students became increasingly annoying to him. He again announced at a faculty meeting that he'd like us to ask kids to remove their hats. "I feel like the Lone Ranger," he said, concerning his one-man war against the hatted students.

But hats were still a low priority. If J. W. wanted hats off, it could happen only if teachers knew that he would have students suspended who were insubordinate when asked to remove a hat.

We approached him and explained the committee philosophy regarding out-of-school suspensions. These only amounted to time spent away in a place where one does not need to posture for peers or staff, but can figure things out. There is no need to lecture, threaten, or humiliate such students, or act as though suspension is anything but a chance for a person to collect his or her thoughts, use his or her brains, and return with a fresh plan for success. We felt that this is a far superior consequence for insubordination because it does several things:

1. It makes it clear to the child that his/her behavior won't be tolerated in this setting.

2. It puts the child back in control, unlike In-School Suspension (ISS), or detention, where school figures are made responsible for the child.

3. It tells to the huge remaining body of kids, 99 percent of whom want to be in school, that they will need to think about how to behave.

4. It involves parents directly and forces them to speak with their kids about which behaviors are OK and which are not.

5. It clearly shows us which kids are simply not capable of adjusting their behavior for our setting; we can then begin the search for alternatives for those few.

Perhaps this was a kind of blackmail. We preferred to see it as compromise. The school year ended with some improvements in our halls, but few of us yet willing to confront hats.

By August, J. W. had committed to dealing harshly with insubordination and other behavioral issues. With input from the Climate Committee, he wrote a list of behavioral expectations for students that specifically mentioned language and insubordination, and the possible consequence of suspension for those offenses. This became part of a booklet describing student expectations and responsibilities, which was mailed to every child in our attendance area. It included a kind of mini-contract—an acknowledgment to be signed by each student and a parent. These acknowledgments would be collected the first week of school. Students who had not returned them in the first week would be called to the office. This show of good faith convinced the Climate Committee that "hats" were important; we urged staff to support J. W.'s insistence that kids not wear them in school. Then we'd see.

Our survey the previous spring had also shown major concerns with language in the building. We began the year with a "keep-it-clean" strategy designed by the Climate Committee. Announcements from our building principals and from kids on the morning TV show stressed the need for everyone to work at curbing this kind of noise pollution. In addition, three Climate members agreed to work after school with kids who continued to use "bad" language, which included not only swearing, but racist terms and sexually suggestive comments, too. All staff were supplied with yellow notices that they could give to students with or without comment. The notices read: *PLEASE KEEP IT CLEAN! You've used inappropriate language. Please do better.* On the sheet, the staff person could indicate the type of inappropriate language that was observed. One copy was given to the student, and one was saved for the committee. When a single name appeared for the second time, a subcommittee member would take time during his or her free period to seek out that child and pull the student briefly from class. In the privacy and quiet of the hall, the student would be questioned about language issues.

Is this the kind of language that makes your parents proud?

Ah, not really.

Do you think we are serious here about cleaning up the language?

Yes.

I'll show you here on the yellow notice what it means if you forget for a third time what appropriate language is in your school. You will meet with a group of teachers after school to decide whether your parents
need to be called, or if you should be given another chance to use more acceptable, grown-up language. Do you think you can avoid a third offense?

Yeah, sure.

We had been assured in advance that our principals would suspend students who continued to use inappropriate language after the three warnings from staff, or who failed to show up at the after-school hearing. Without this assurance, the program could still have been effective, but not many teachers would have confronted language. If you wish to have a "clean" school, your principals must do this much.

The "keep-it-clean" system took up many committee-member hours in the first weeks of the new school year, but the effect was dramatic. Language vastly improved, with no involvement by the office. After-school sessions with kids were held only a few times. Staff had cooperated in confronting language and were seeing the results. Teachers inhabited the halls between classes. Kids walked and talked with less cynicism. Vandalism decreased. We all felt better.

It was easy, then, to institute the Valley Fair trip. It had long been my dream to celebrate the end of the year by seeing our school visit the grand amusement park in Shakopee, Minnesota sometime during the final week. I soon realized that a more realistic aim was to take the ninth-grade class, and to offer a special party that day at school for the remaining eighth- and seventh-grade classes. Improvements in the school climate were so pronounced by this time that many staff volunteered to organize special events for the eighth and seventh grades, who were assured that we would attempt to make Valley Fair a tradition they might enjoy as ninth graders.

By this time, the efforts of the Climate Committee and our staff and administrators were getting the attention of the community, especially of the Parents, Teachers, Students Association (PTSA), which had formed in a hurry after the racial incident. These were observant, savvy, enthusiastic citizens who pledged to help our staff in any way. They planned and organized fund-raisers that made it possible for all ninth-grade students to attend Valley Fair at a cost of only $5 per person.

The board approved our plan, and after that, we wrote to the city for a grant. We emphasized the behavioral incentives of this trip—Any student who avoided a referral for insubordination in the last six weeks of the school year, and who had the approval of his/her teachers, would be eligible to attend.

The school population was amazed. Kids began cautioning other kids: "If you swing at him, Robby, you'll miss the trip." Fights and other springtime rites of mischief—cutting classes, squirt guns, and so on—became far more infrequent.

On a beautiful clear day in June, I clamored to be one of the first from our school to ride the steep-dropping roller coaster, the Excalibur, at Valley Fair. The kids behaved beautifully for all events.

If you want a clean and comfortable school where kids and staff feel respected, you must begin with:

- staff that is interested in changing or improving the present school, and a principal who is not afraid to explain specifically to parents and the community at large that their school needs change;

- an active parent group, one that will help raise funds to send kids on roller coasters and field trips to the sewage treatment plant, and that will put a shiny red apple in the mailbox of each teacher, administrator, custodian, secretary, cook, and aide;

- frequent and honest communication with parents;

- clear definition of insubordination and assurance to staff that students will never be excused for mocking or defying them;

- a philosophy that says "education is a privilege we proudly offer to our young people";

- emphasis that school is not the street, and insistence that it remains separate from the toys and noise of the street; and

- staff who agree to teach in the halls.

I know this much—With good people acting decisively from the top down and good people acting in support of them from the bottom up, you can have any school you want.

Final Days

Jake stormed out of his math class during review for the final test. Mr. B. had refused Jake's request to use the bathroom. He knew Jake had eaten lunch the previous period and had enjoyed ample time to sort out his needs. Moreover, school policy discourages teachers from giving hall passes the last few days of school. Mr. B. had supported such administrative requests for the past 42 years. In three days, he would retire.

As Jake left the room, he blurted out an obscenity. Mr. B wrote a disciplinary referral, and

Jake was subsequently suspended out of school a day and then given in-school suspension for one day when he came back.

I had enjoyed every day with Jake this year. He was very quick verbally, insightful in his responses, energetic, and eager to please. He'd earned Bs the whole year. It hurt me that he'd insulted a friend and colleague, and (I hope) embarrassed himself. During my preparation period I carried this note to him in the ISS (In-School Suspension):

Dear Jake,

I offer these questions in friendship. I'm sorry you made some trouble. Have you apologized to Mr. B.? He's been dealing with tantrums for 40-some years, while helping some 12,000 or 13,000 kids learn math. He is retiring this year, and I would much prefer he would remember your sincere apology than your hissy fit. I hope you feel the same way.

Have you apologized to your parents? I know they did not raise you to insult and despise people who don't give you your way. (<u>I had taught six of Jake's eight brothers.</u>) Like it or not, for your whole life your behavior will represent your folks. Every day of your life until you die is a reflection on your parents and how you were raised. I hope you'll apologize to them for acting so far below the standards they've set for you.

You've been one of my favorite people this year, Jake. That's why I'm taking time for this, hoping you are willing to take a look at what you need to do if you are ever going to become a real man.

Sincerely,
Mr. Mahle

I don't know if Jake apologized; I don't know if he's a man today, or becoming one in any way. I do know that kids' screw-ups (and our own) offer us opportunities to improve how we've been teaching. It didn't take long to write a note to Jake and let him know one man's view of how boys evolve into men. Men and other mature adults finish what they start.

How we finish the year is more important, in my mind, than how we started it. Day one is crucial, as it sets the tone for our work over the next nine months. But the last day is even more critical—for how we and the kids exit will cast an air over everything we've done in this season of teaching. We want to feel good about the year and move happily into summer. We want to return in the fall to the best job in the world.

Preparing kids for the last few days requires careful planning. And every "last day" has taught me something new for the next. On the last day of my first year, I handed back papers my eighth graders had written. I knew this would involve them in reading and sharing with each other, and enjoying seeing what progress they'd made. They did enjoy the hour—and especially enjoyed fashioning paper airplanes, which sailed frequently through windows open in to the bright June day. A few enterprising youngsters tore their papers into tiny confetti bits that settled on me like snowflakes at the moment of dismissal as I trailed the kids down the stairwell from my room on the third floor. Others waited until they were outside to celebrate. Driving home later that day, I found papers floating around blocks away, stopped to pick up a few, and saw my name and a date in the upper right hand corner, just where I'd taught my students to write them, neatly and in ink. It took several years to regain the good graces of the custodians after that first-year debacle.

That first year I'd resisted any attempt to organize a room party or celebration. I thought those easy teachers who'd brought popcorn and soda for the kids were pretty foolish. Anyhow, the next year I designed a four-day final test that would involve kids in a variety of activities and keep their attention. When I explained the test, I showed how positive participation was the key. Anyone could show an A on their report card for the "final test" if they were positive and courteous. I began with a point system of 25 per day, for a total of a 100, and a tight grading scale that required 95 for an A, 90 for a B, and 85 for a C. I wasn't going to give Ds. Students would receive five points for being on time, two for bringing materials, three if they did not ask for a pass to leave the room, and so on, with two to five points given for each activity I'd scheduled that period. I had kids perform skits, read favorite poems, write poems, even read silently for half of one period while I figured out my grades.

The last day, each student wrote a letter to me and a thank-you note to one or more of the other staff who'd helped them in some way.

Dear Mr. Tiny,

You probably don't remember me but when I started junior high I was a very little person. You are maybe the biggest person I've ever seen. Anyhow, my first day in 7th grade I couldn't get my locker open at the end of the day and I knew the bus was loading and I would miss it. It was raining and I needed my jacket, plus my math book because we got an assignment that first day and I didn't want to be the one screw-up who didn't get it done. So I needed my locker open, bad. You saw me trying so hard, probably just about in tears, and you came over with your locker key just in time. I'll never forget that. And on my last day of school here, I want to thank you for making my first day here a success.

Sincerely yours,
Bena S.
9th grade graduate

I provided a checklist of things that each student needed to do during this final week, and had each of them mark the sheet at the end of the period. Final dismissal each day was worth five points. I gave back papers on the first day of the four-day final with the understanding that any paper found outside the classroom would cost the writer 25 points. "I can recognize the handwriting of each of you, too," I reminded them. With the papers, I sent notes home to parents. Parents needed to acknowledge receipt of the papers in order for students to earn five points of the final test. Out of 150 students, all but 10 earned As, and I had only two Fs.

On the last day of my second year, everything had gone along famously until our floor was dismissed. The kids were lined up behind me in the room, waiting for me to lead them out. I took one step into the hall and felt a harsh blow from behind; Rod H. had bolted through the door and rammed into me. "I'm outta here, suckers!"—and, indeed, he was several yards ahead and descending the stairs. I'll always remember Rod for that—not for the great job he'd done on my track team and his steady work in English, but for slamming past his classmates and me in some bold testosterone rush to show how he was a little more free than anyone else. I felt the blow of his passing; a smaller person would likely have been injured.

The next year, I announced that dismissal would be from one's assigned seat, and I increased the all-important dismissal points to 15 for the last day. Students can learn and thrive the last few days and enjoy their final moments with you. They will remember that you never wilted, never folded in on their whiny little pleas:

Can we go early? Pleeeeeeeease M-i-s-t-e-r M-a-h-l-e? Can we? Can we?

Tell you what.

What, what!

You sit quietly in your seat before the dismissal of our floor is announced by the office, and when it is announced, I'll let you go early.

Really?

You bet.

Wait a minute. That's not early. That's on time.

Oh. OK. Then I'll let you go on time. I love you. Have a safe summer!

Looney, looney, looney. . . .

A Decade in the Classroom

After my tenth year of beginning and ending school years, I felt compelled to summarize some of what I learned along the way in writing. I offer you the following essay and hope it will help.

To survive teaching, it will help to remember: *Never underestimate the capabilities of kids.* Some love to play dumb in order that you won't expect much from them. Expect it anyhow. Don't be shy about pestering them some. A few will do the work just to escape your bugging them about it.

Secondly, never allow kids to insult you, themselves, your colleagues, or each other. It is your job to help kids become good people as well as good students. Youngsters often feel ugly and dumb; some would like others to keep them company in those feelings. By not allowing put-downs, we free up brain space for thoughts about a hypotenuse, or what a black, midnight raven might mean to a sorrowful man.

Third, be aware of the power you have to bring about appropriate behavior. A student who breaks pencils and stuffs the fragments up her nose is asking you for something. A few words after class with her may help you learn what it is. Don't hesitate either to seek an alliance with parents and counselors; they want to know you and work with you. Parents of negative children may well have had poor school experiences themselves; be patient and encouraging with them and believe that they don't want their children to continue with inappropriate behavior.

Relax a little bit. Lighten up. Back off. Laugh.

Stop blaming yourself when kids don't always learn as you hoped they would. Despite Herculean efforts, some youngsters will be preoccupied with thoughts about their parents' divorce or the aches and soreness that appear in joints and tissues that adults casually say are "just growing pains." A kid knows it's cancer. He knows, too, that his braces hurt, and that he looks dorky in his new jeans. He knows Emmett is going to get his gang after him, and that the brown-eyed girl he likes thinks he's a wussie. So if you don't see their lights turn on today, simply try again tomorrow. After all, the next day a student is older, a bit more mature. You may succeed with him then.

Finally, respect kids and they will respect you back. Remind them often that they are important and valuable individuals who, if they learn properly, will one day have good jobs and pay taxes which will support you in your old age.

Each of us can survive and stay sane in the teaching game if we stick up for ourselves and the youngsters we teach, and if we allow them to nurture and amaze us with their special talents and charms. I know it's possible because I've been doing it for ten years (over 27 now), and I'm not looney, looney, looney.

■   ■   ■

Afterward

A few weeks ago, I was visiting a friend and reading a newsletter I'd found on her coffee table. I read a quotation from Margaret Meade on the front page: <u>A folk song could save the world.</u> It made me pause, as though I'd just heard a song lyric that explained love or the meaning of life. I knew I'd have to write about it later, as writing is one way I make sense of thoughts and problems that stick in my mind.

<u>A folk song could save the world.</u> Well, what about that? Though nothing I say here may mean anything, anything could mean something, and anyhow, everything left unsaid comes to nothing. So why not write or talk about folk songs? Because if you are at all like me, then you've watched <u>60 Minutes</u> and heard that ticking clock. That incessant ticking creates an urgency. Could it be my sense that I, a guy who believes that writing is such a powerful tool, should write the folk song that will save the world?

I think all teachers believe at some point that they can save the world. It takes a few years to settle on making a difference. But we can opt for hope and agree with the quote. For we know that a folk song contains lyrics that appeal to folks—sentiments that most folks can understand and that play to hearts with a common sense of what is reasonable and what is right in life. That is what a good folk song does. A good one. I couldn't write it, probably, but I can listen for it and share when I think I've found it. And I hope we will all believe it is out there some-where, collecting just the right words to blend in harmony with the universal tick of our good hearts.

A Final Note

Author Benj Mahle would greatly appreciate hearing your comments and/or suggestions regarding the material presented in *More Power Teaching*. He can be contacted via e-mail at:

Hyperlink
bmahle@esc.rochester.k12.mn.us

He can also be reached at his school address:

Mr. Benj Mahle
c/o Century High School
2525 Viola Road Northeast
Rochester, MN 55906

Mr. Mahle is available to conduct weekend and summer workshops based on *More Power Teaching* and his first book, *Power Teaching*, published by Good Apple. For information about his presentations, he can be reached at the addresses above.